THE
ITALIAN COOK BOOK

THE

ITALIAN COOK BOOK

The Art of Eating Well

PRACTICAL RECIPES

OF THE

ITALIAN CUISINE

PASTRIES
SWEETS, FROZEN DELICACIES
AND SYRUPS

COMPILED BY

MRS. MARIA GENTILE

KALPAZ

ISBN: 978-93-5128-395-9(HB)

First Published in 1919
Indian Reprint in 2017

Published by

Kalpaz Publications
C-30, Satyawati Nagar,
Delhi – 110052
E-mail: kalpaz@hotmail.com
Website: kalpazpublications.com
Ph.: +91-9212142040

Cataloging in Publication Data—DK

Courtesy: D.K. Agencies (P) Ltd. <docinfo@dkagencies.com>

The Italian cook book : the art of eating well : practical recipes of the Italian cuisine : pastries, sweets, frozen delicacies and syrups / compiled by Mrs. Maria Gentile.
pages cm

"First published in 1919"
Includes index.

ISBN 9789351283959 (HB)

1. Cooking, Italian. 2. Cookbooks. lcgft I. Gentile, Maria (Cook book compiler), compiler.

LCC TX723.G45 2017 | DDC 641.5945 23

PREFACE

One of the beneficial results of the Great War has been the teaching of thrift to the American housewife. For patriotic reasons and for reasons of economy, more attention has been bestowed upon the preparing and cooking of food that is to be at once palatable, nourishing and economical.

In the Italian **cuisine** we find in the highest degree these three qualities. That it is palatable, all those who have partaken of food in an Italian **trattoria** or at the home of an Italian family can testify, that it is healthy the splendid manhood and womanhood of Italy is a proof more than sufficient. And who could deny, knowing the thriftiness of the Italian race, that it is economical?

It has therefore been thought that a book of PRACTICAL RECIPES OF THE ITALIAN CUISINE could be offered to the American public with hope of success. It is not a pretentious book, and the recipes have been made as clear and simple as possible. Some of the dishes described are not peculiar to Italy. All, however, are representative of the **Cucina Casalinga** of the peninsular Kingdom, which is not the least product of a lovable and simple people, among whom the art of living well and getting the most out of life at a moderate expense has been attained to a very high degree.

1

BROTH OR SOUP STOCK

(Brodo)

To obtain good broth the meat must be put in cold water, and then allowed to boil slowly. Add to the meat some pieces of bones and "soup greens" as, for instance, celery, carrots and parsley. To give a brown color to the broth, some sugar, first browned at the fire, then diluted in cold water, may be added.

While it is not considered that the broth has much nutritive power, it is excellent to promote the digestion. Nearly all the Italian soups are made on a basis of broth.

A good recipe for substantial broth to be used for invalids is the following: Cut some beef in thin slices and place them in a large saucepan; add some salt. Pour cold water upon them, so that they are entirely covered. Cover the saucepan so that it is hermetically closed and place on the cover a receptacle containing water, which must be constantly renewed. Keep on a low fire for six hours, then on a strong fire for ten minutes. Strain the liquid in cheese cloth.

The soup stock, besides being used for soups, is a necessary ingredient in hundreds of Italian dishes.

2

SOUP OF "CAPPELLETTI"

This Soup is called of "**Cappelletti**" or "little hats" on account of the shape of the "**Cappelletti.**"

First a thin sheet of paste is made according to the following directions:

The best and most tender paste is made simply of eggs, flour and salt, water may be substituted for part of the eggs, for economy, or when a less rich paste is needed. Allow about a cup of flour to an egg. Put the flour on a bread board, make a hollow in the middle and break in the egg. Use any extra whites that are on hand. Knead it thoroughly, adding more flour if necessary, until you have a paste you can roll out. Roll it as thin as an eighth of an inch. A long rolling pin is necessary, but any stick, well scrubbed and sand papered, will serve in lieu of the long Italian rolling pin.

Cut from this sheet of paste rounds measuring about three inches in diameter. In the middle of each circle place a spoonful of filling that must be made beforehand, composed of cooked meat (chicken, pork or veal) ground very fine and seasoned with grated cheese, grated lemon peel, nutmeg, allspice, salt. The ground meat is to be mixed with an equal amount of curds or cottage cheese.

When the filling is placed in the circle of paste, fold the latter over and moisten the edge of the paste with the finger dipped in water to make it stay securely closed.

These **cappelletti** should be cooked in chicken or beef broth until the paste is tender, and served with this broth as a soup.

3

BREAD SOUP

(Panata)

This excellent and nutritious soup is a godsend for using the stale bread that must never again be thrown away. It is composed of bread crumbs and grated bread, eggs, grated cheese, nutmeg (in very small quantity) and salt, all mixed together and put in broth previously prepared, which must be warm at the moment of the immersion, but not at the boiling point. Then place it on a low fire and stir gently. Any vegetable left over may be added.

4

GNOCCHI

This is an excellent soup, but as it requires boiled or roast breast of chicken or turkey it is well to make it only when these ingredients are handy.

Prepare a certain quantity of boiled potatoes, the mealy kind being preferred. Mash the potatoes and mix them with chicken or turkey breast well ground, grated cheese (Parmesan or Swiss), two or more yolks of eggs, salt and a small quantity of nutmeg. Pour the compound on the bread board with a quantity of flour sufficient to make a paste and roll it in little sticks as thick as the small finger. Cut the sticks in little pieces about half an inch long and put them in boiling water. Five or six minutes' cooking will be sufficient.

5

VEGETABLE SOUP

(Zuppa Santè)

Any kind of vegetables may be used for this soup: carrots, celery, cabbage, turnips, onions, potatoes, spinach, the outside leaves of lettuce or greens of any variety.

Select three or four kind of vegetables, shred or chop coarsely cabbage or greens, and slice or cut in cubes the root vegetables. Put them over the fire with a small quantity of cooking oil or butter substitute, and let them fry until they have absorbed the fat. Then add broth and cook until the vegetables are very tender. Fry croutons of stale bread in oil and serve them in the soup.

6

QUEEN'S SOUP

(Zuppa Regina)

This is made with the white meat of chicken, which is to be ground in a meat grinder together with blanched almonds (5 or 6) for one quart of chicken. stock. To the meat and almond add some bread crumbs, first soaked in milk or broth, in the proportion of about one fifth of the quantity of the meat. All these ingredients are to be rubbed to a very smooth paste and hot broth is to be added to them. If you wish the soup to be richer and have a more milky consistency, use the yolk of an egg, which should be beaten, and have a few tablespoonfuls of hot broth stirred into it before adding to the soup. Do not let the soup boil after the egg is added or it will curdle.

One slice of stale bread may be cut into cubes, fried in deep fat, and the croutons put in the soup. Send it to the table with a dish of grated cheese.

7

BEAN SOUP

(Zuppa di fagiuoli)

One cup of dried beans, kidney, navy or lima is to be soaked over night. Then boil until tender. It is preferable to put the beans to cook in cold water with a pinch of soda. When they come to boil, pour off this water and add fresh.

Chop fine ¼ onion, one clove of garlic, one sprig of parsley and one piece of celery and put them to fry in ¼ cup of oil with salt and a generous amount of pepper. When the vegetables are a delicate brown add to them two cups of the broth from the beans and 1 cup of tomatoes (canned or fresh). Let all come to a boil and pour the mixture into the kettle of beans from which some of the water has been drained, if they are very liquid. This soup may be served as it is or rubbed through a sieve before serving. Croutons or triangles of dry toast make an excellent addition.

The bean soup is made without meat or chicken broth, and it belongs consequently to that class of soup called by the Italians "Minestra di Màgro" or "lean soup, to be served preferably on Friday and other days in which the Roman Catholic Church prohibits the use of meats.

8

LENTIL SOUP

(Zuppa di lenticchie)

The lentil soup is prepared in the same way as the bean soup, only substituting lentils for beans. A good combination is that of lentils and rice. The nutritive qualities of the lentils are not sufficiently known in this country, but all books on dietetics speak very highly of them.

9

VEGETABLE CHOWDER

(Minestrone alla Milanese)

Cut off the rind of ½ lb. salt pork and put it into two quarts of water to boil. Cut off a small slice of the pork and beat it to a paste with two or three sprigs of parsley, a little celery and one kernel of garlic. Add this paste to the pork and water. Slice two carrots, cut the rib out of the leaves of ¼ medium sized cabbage. Add the carrots, cabbage leaves, other vegetables, seasoning and butter to the soup, and let it boil slowly for 2½ hours. The last ½ hour add one small handful of rice for each person.

When the pork is very soft, remove and slice in little ribbons and put it back.

The minestrone is equally good eaten cold.

10

RAVIOLI

Put on the bread board about two pounds of flour in a heap; make a hollow in the middle and put in it a piece of butter, three egg-yolks, salt and three or four tablespoonfuls of lukewarm water. Make a paste and knead it well, then let it stand for an hour, wrapped or covered with a linen cloth. Then spread the paste to a thin sheet, as thin as a ten-cent piece.

11

Chop and grind pieces of roast or boiled chicken meat: add to it an equal part of marrow from the bones of beef and pieces of brains, three yolks, some crumbs of bread soaked in milk or broth and some grated cheese (Parmesan or Swiss). Rub through a sieve and make little balls as big as a hazel-nut, which are to be placed at equal distances (a little more than an inch) in a line over the sheet of paste.

Beat a whole egg and pass it over the paste with a brush all around the little balls. Cover these with another sheet of paste, press down the intervals between each ball, and then separate each section from the other with a knife. Moisten the edges of each section with the finger dipped in cold water, to make them stick together, and press them down with the fingers or the prongs of a fork. Then put to boil in water seasoned with salt or, better still, in broth. The ravioli are then to be served hot seasoned with cheese and butter or with brown stock or tomato sauce.

11

PAVESE SOUP

(Zuppa alla Pavese)

Cut as many thin slices of bread as are needed in order that each person may have at least two of them. These slices are then to be toasted and browned with butter. Poach two eggs for each person, one on each slice of bread and place the slices on a large and deep dish (not in a soup tureen). Pour hot broth in the plate, taking care not to break the eggs, season with Parmesan or Swiss cheese, and serve.

PASTE

SPAGHETTI, MACARONI ETC.

(Pasta Asciutta)

The Italians serve the spaghetti or macaroni at the beginning of the meal, in place of soup, and they give it the name of **Minestra Asciutta** or "dry" soup. Besides the familiar spaghetti, the paste is served in many other forms and with different seasoning. This is by far the most popular Italian dish, and it seems to have pleased the taste of all the peoples of the earth. The highly nutritive qualities of spaghetti and of cheese, their indispensable condiment, have been recognized by all diet authorities and, as for its palatableness, the lovers of spaghetti are just as enthusiastic and numerous outside of Italy as within the boundaries of that blessed country. The most popular seasoning for spaghetti, are tomato sauce, brown stock and anchovy sauce. The description of these three condiments follows:

12

TOMATO SAUCE

(Salsa di Pomidoro)

Chop together, fine, one quarter of an onion, a clove of garlic, a piece of celery as long as your finger, a few bay leaves and just enough parsley. Season with a little oil, salt and pepper, cut up seven or eight tomatoes and put everything over the fire together. Stir it from time to time and when you see the juice condensing into a thin custard strain through a sieve, and it is ready for use.

When fresh tomatoes are not available the tomato paste may be used. This is a concentrated paste made from tomatoes and spices which is to be had, at all Italian grocers', now so numerous in all American cities. Thinned with water, it is a much used ingredient in Italian recipes. Catsup and concentrated tomato soup do not make satisfactory substitutes as they are too sweet in flavor. Of course canned tomatoes seasoned with salt and a bit of bay leaf, can always be used instead of fresh tomatoes.

This sauce serves many purposes. It is good on boiled meat; excellent to dress macaroni, spaghetti or other pastes which have been seasoned with butter and cheese, or on boiled rice seasoned in the same way (see Risotto). Mushrooms are a fine addition to it.

When using concentrated paste the following recipes will be found to give good results:

Chop one onion, one carrot and a celery stalk: form a little bunch of parsley and other aromatic greens and put everything to brown in a saucepan together with a piece of butter. Add a reasonable portion of tomato paste while cooking, stir and keep on a low fire until the sauce assumes the necessary consistency.

13

BROWN STOCK

(Sugo di Carne)

Cover the bottom of a saucepan with thin slices of beef taken from a juicy cut and small pieces of salt pork. Place over a large onion, one carrot, and a stalk of celery, all chopped in small pieces. Add some butter and cover the whole with any trimmings from steaks or roasts and any bit of left over cooked meat. Season with salt and cloves. Put over the fire without stirring. When you smell the onions getting very brown, turn the meat and when everything is quite brown add a cup of water, renewing the latter three times. Finally add a certain quantity of boiling water or, better still, of broth, and let it boil gently five or six hours. Strain, cool and skim off the fat which will form a cake on top of the liquid.

The meat can be used afterward for meat balls or Croquettes. The stock may be kept for some days and forms the basis for many dishes.

14

ANCHOVY SAUCE

(Salsa d'Acciughe)

This recipe does not call for the filets of anchovies prepared for **hors d'œuvre,** but the less expensive and larger whole anchovies in salt to be had in bulk or cans at large dealers. Wash them thoroughly in plenty of water. Remove head, toil, backbone and skin and they are ready for use.

Put five or six anchovies into a colander and dip quickly into boiling water to loosen the skins, remove the salt, skin and bone them. Chop them and put over the fire in a saucepan with a generous quantity of oil and some pepper. Do not let them boil, but when they are hot add two tablespoons of butter and three or four tablespoons of concentrated tomato juice made by cooking down canned tomatoes and rubbing through a sieve. When this sauce is used to season spaghetti, these must be boiled in water that is only slightly salted and care must be taken not to let them become too soft. The quantities above mentioned ought to be sufficient for about one pound of spaghetti.

15

SPAGHETTI OR MACARONI WITH BUTTER AND CHEESE

(Pasta al burro e formaggio)

This is the simplest form in which the spaghetti may be served, and it is generally reserved for the thickest paste. The spaghetti are to be boiled until tender in salted water, taking care to remove them when tender, and not cooked until they lose form. They should not be put into the water until this is at a boiling point.

Take as much macaroni as will half fill the dish in which it is to be served. Break into pieces two and a half to three inches long if you so desire. The Italians leave them unbroken, but their skill in turning them around the fork and eating them is not the privilege of everybody. Put the macaroni into salted boiling water, and boil twelve to fifteen minutes, or until the macaroni is perfectly soft. Stir frequently to prevent the macaroni from adhering to the bottom. Turn it into a colander to drain; then put it into a pudding-dish with a generous quantity of butter and grated cheese. If more cheese is liked, it can be brought to the table so that the guests can help themselves to it.

The macaroni called "Mezzani" which is a name designating size, not quality, is the preferable kind for macaroni dishes made with butter and cheese.

16

MACARONI WITH SAUCE

(Maccheroni al sugo)

The most appreciated kind of macaroni are those seasoned with tomato sauce or with brown stock (see nos. 12 and 13). The macaroni are boiled as above, then drained in a colander, returned to the saucepan and mixed with the sauce and grated cheese. For those who like it some butter may be added in the mixing.

17

MACARONI WITH ANCHOVY SAUCE

(Maccheroni con salsa d'acciughe)

After the paste is drained thoroughly it is to be put into the hot dish in which it is to be served and the anchovy sauce poured over it and well mixed with two silver forks until the sauce has gone all through it. Some olive oil may be added, but grated cheese is not generally used with the anchovy sauce.

18

MACARONI A LA CORINNA

(Maccheroni alla Corinna)

Put on the fire a pot with two quarts of salted water to which add a small piece of butter. When it begins to boil put in it ¾ lb. macaroni. Let it boil for five minutes, then drain them in a colander. Put them again in new boiling water, prepared as above and let them cook on a slow fire. Drain them again. Cover the bottom of a plate with macaroni and cover this first layer with grated cheese and with some vegetables in macèdoine, that is, chopped fine and fried brown with butter. Repeat the draining, moisten the macaroni with the water in which they have previously cooked and keep on a low fire for ten minutes more.

The Macèdoine of vegetables can be made with a dozen Bruxelles sprouts or one cabbage, half a dozen big asparagus cut in little pieces, a carrot cut in thin slices, a dozen small onions, some turnips and half a dozen mushrooms. The mushrooms and the asparagus can be omitted. Melt some butter in a saucepan and when the turnips, the carrots and the onions are half cooked, add the cabbage or sprouts. Put in some water and some more butter, boil for ten minutes and then add the mushrooms and the asparagus, adding salt and pepper, and a little sugar if this is desired.

19

MACARONI "AU GRATIN"

(Maccheroni al gratin)

Boil the macaroni in salted water until tender and drain them. Butter slightly a fireproof casserole and lay on the bottom some grated cheese and grated bread. Alternate the layers of cheese with macaroni and on the top layer of macaroni put more cheese and bread grated. Over the whole pour some melted butter, cover the casserole, (or pyrex plate) and put it in the oven with a low fire. Keep for ten minutes or more, until the top appears browned.

20

MACARONI NAPOLITAINE

(Maccheroni alla Napoletana)

Grind 1/4 lb. salt pork or bacon and fry it out in a saucepan. While it is frying put one small onion through the grinder. As soon as the pork begins to brown add the onion, the parsley chopped, a clove (or small section) of garlic shredded fine, and a few dried mushrooms which have been softened by soaking in warm water. When the vegetables are very brown (great care must be taken not to burn the onion, which scorches very easily) add 1/2 lb. round steak ground coarsely or cut up in little cubes. When the meat is a good brown color, add some fresh or canned tomatoes or half a tablespoonful of tomato paste and simmer slowly until all has cooked down to a thick creamy sauce. It will probably take 3/4 hour. The sauce may be bound together with a little flour if it shows a tendency to separate.

This sauce is used to dress all kinds of macaroni and spaghetti, also for boiled rice (see Risotto). The macaroni or spaghetti should be left unbroken when cooked. If they are too long to fit in the kettle immerse one end in the boiling salted water and in a very few minutes the ends of the spaghetti under the water will become softened so that the rest can be pushed down into the kettle. Be careful not to overcook it, and it will not be pasty, but firm and tender. Drain it carefully and put in a hot soup tureen. Sprinkle a handful of grated cheese over it and pour on the sauce. Lift with two forks until thoroughly mixed.

21

MACARONI FRIED WITH OIL

(Maccheroni all'olio)

After the macaroni have boiled drain them and put them in a saucepan in which some good olive oil has already boiled, with a clove of garlic chopped fine. Let the paste fry, taking care that it doesn't stick to the bottom of the saucepan, and when it is well browned on one side, turn it to have the other side browned. Serve the macaroni very hot. Add no cheese.

22

RISOTTO MILANAISE

(Risotto alla Milanese)

Melt a small piece of butter in a saucepan. Brown in the butter a medium sized onion, cut in thin slices. When the onion is browned, take it away from the saucepan and add little by little the rice, stirring it with a wooden spoon. Every time that the rice becomes dry, add some hot broth (or hot water) until the rice is completely cooked. Add salt and pepper and a little saffron, if you like it.

When the rice is almost cooked, add to it some brown stock. Dress with parmesan cheese and some butter. Mix well and serve hot. This dish must not be allowed to be overcooked or cooled before eating.

23

RISOTTO WITH CHICKEN GIBLETS

(Risotto alla Milanese II)

The broth for this risotto may be made by cooking together the giblets, neck and tips of wings of a chicken which is to be roasted, or it may be made from the left-overs of roast fowl.

Boil the rice until it is about half done in salted water. Then let the water cook away and begin adding the broth, in such quantity that the rice will be nearly dry when it is tender. Fry one chopped onion in the oil or fat. Some mushrooms cut up small are a very good addition to this "Soffritto." Mince the chicken giblets and add to the onion. Stir the mixture into the rice. Add grated cheese and a beaten egg just as the rice is taken from the fire.

24

(Risotto con piselli)

Wash and dry 1½ lb. rice; chop fine one medium sized onion and put it on the fire with a small quantity of butter.

When the onion is well browned, add the rice little by little, stirring with a wooden spoon. Add some boiling water one cup at a time. Drain the peas previously prepared (fresh or canned peas may be used) and add them toward the end of the cooking. When the whole is almost cooked, add some salt and take it away from the water almost dry. Add some butter, stir and serve hot.

25

RISOTTO WITH LOBSTER

(Risotto coi gamberi)

For this risotto either lobster or crab meat can be used: the former is, however, considered more tasty. The lobster or crab meat ought to be about half the weight of the rice employed. A little more than a pound of rice and half this weight of crab meat ought to be enough for six persons.

Chop fine a sprig of parsley, a stalk of celery, one carrot, half an onion a clove of garlic and brown the whole in good olive oil. When browned, add the crab meat and season with salt and pepper. During the cooking process stir and turn over the crabs, and when they have become red, pour over as much hot water as is necessary to cook the rice.

After the water boils for a while, remove the lobster (or crab, or craw-fish) leaving the saucepan on the fire. Put half of the crabs aside, and grind the rest. Rub the ground meat through the sieve and put it back on the fire. In another saucepan melt some butter and put into it little by little the rice that has been washed and dried. Stir and add the broth from the first saucepan. When the rice is almost cooked add the craw-fish that you have put aside, or rather its meat extracted from the shells, take from the fire and pour over it the fish mixture, adding some grated cheese.

26

RICE WITH SAFFRON

(Riso alla Milanese con Zafferano)

Wash and dry the rice and put it in boiling broth (beef or chicken broth). When the rice is half cooked add half its weight of marrow of beef bone, cut into small pieces. A few minutes are sufficient for the cooking of the marrow. Add grated cheese and remove the kettle from the fire.

Dissolve some saffron in one or two tablespoonfuls of broth; sift it through a sieve and mix with rice, which is to be served very hot, and makes an excellent soup.

27
RICE CAKES
(Frittelle di riso)

Cook the rice in milk, adding a small quantity of butter, some salt, half a teaspoon of sugar and just a taste of lemon peel. Let the rice cool down after being thoroughly cooked, then add three yolks of eggs (for 1/4 lb. of rice) and some flour. Mix well and let the whole rest for several hours. When about to fry, beat the white of the eggs to a froth, add to the rice mixing slowly, and put into the saucepan with a ladle.

28
FRIED ARTICHOKE
(Carciofi fritti)

Take two artichokes, cut out the hard part of the leaves and of the stalk, cut them in two. Then cut these halves into section or slices so as to have eight or ten for each artichoke, according to size. As you cut them, throw them into cold water and when they are well washed, dry them, but not thoroughly, putting them at once into the flour so that the latter remains attached to it. Beat the white of an egg, but not to a froth, then mix the yolk with the white and salt the whole. Shake out the artichokes to take away the superfluous flour and then put them in the egg, leaving them for a while so that the egg may be attached to them.

Throw the pieces one by one into the pan where there is boiling fat, butter or olive oil, and when they are well browned, take them away and serve with lemon. If it is desired that the artichokes remain white, it is better to fry them in oil and to squeeze half lemon into the water where the artichokes are put to soften.

29

STEAMED ARTICHOKES

(Carciofi a vapore)

Artichokes have been only recently imported to the United States, principally by Italian farmers, and they are just beginning to find their way into the American kitchen. The artichokes may be eaten raw or cooked. It is a healthy and palatable vegetable, easily digested when cooked. It is nutritious and adapted for convalescents. It may be prepared in a thousand ways, and here follow some of the simplest and most tasteful.

To prepare the steamed artichokes they must

first be cleaned and the stalk cut to less than half an inch. Put them in a saucepan, standing on their bottoms, one near the other, in half an inch or more of water. In an opening made in the middle put salt and pepper, and pour inside as much good olive oil as they may contain. Cover well the saucepan and put it on the fire. The artichokes, that are already seasoned, will be cooked by the steam.

30

STEWED ARTICHOKES

(Carciofi in stufato)

Wash the artichokes and cut the hard part of the leaves (the top). Widen the leaves and insert a hash composed of bread crumbs, parsely, salt, pepper and oil. Place the artichokes in the saucepan standing on their stalk, one touching the other. Cover them with water and let them cook for two hours or more. When the leaves are easily detached they are cooked.

31

ARTICHOKES WITH BUTTER

(Carciofi al burro)

Wash, dry and cut out the top of the leaves of as many artichokes as are needed. Cut them in two or four and boil them in salt water. When tender, drain them, have them slightly browned in melted butter and season with salt and pepper.

When served in a vegetable dish or placed in a pyramid on a round plate, sprinkle with grated cheese.

32

FRIED SQUASH

(Zucchine fritte)

The squashes used by Italians for frying and other purposes are very small, and for this reason they are called "Zucchine" or small squashes. They can be bought at those shops kept by Italian vegetable dealers that are now to be found in large number in most American cities and, invariably, in Italian neighborhoods during the summer season. The "Zucchine" are an extremely tasty vegetable and they are especially good when fried.

Select the squashes that are long and thin: wash them cut them in little strips less than half an inch thick. Take away the softer part of the interior and salt moderately. Leave them aside for an hour or two, then drain them but don't dry them. Put them in flour and rub gently in a sieve to take away the superfluous flour: immediately after put them in a saucepan where there is already oil, fat or butter boiling. At the beginning don't touch them to avoid breaking, and only when they have become a little hardened stir them and remove when they begin to be browned.

33

LAMB OMELET

(Agnello in frittata)

Cut in little pieces a loin of lamb, which is the part that lends itself best for this dish, and fry in lard: a little quantity of lard is sufficient, because the meat of the loins is rather fat. When half cooked season with salt and pepper and when fully cooked pour over four or five whole eggs slightly beaten also seasoned moderately with salt and pepper. Mix, taking care that the eggs do not harden.

34

FRIED CHICKEN

(Pollo fritto)

Wash a spring chicken and keep in boiling water for one minute. Cut into pieces at the joints, roll them in flour, season with salt and pepper and dip in two whole beaten eggs. After leaving the pieces of chicken for half an hour, roll them in bread crumbs, repeating the operation twice if necessary. Put into a saucepan with boiling oil or fat, seeing that the pieces of chicken are well browned on both sides. Keep the fire low. Serve hot with lemon.

35

CHICKEN ALLA CACCIATORA

(Pollo alla cacciatora)

Chop one large onion and keep it for more than half an hour in cold water, then dry it and brown it aside. Cut up a chicken, sprinkle the pieces with flour, salt and pepper and sautè in the fat which remains in the frying pan. When the chicken is brown add one pint fresh or canned tomatoes and half a dozen sweet green peppers and put back the onion. When the gravy is thick enough add hot water to prevent the burning of the vegetables. Cover the pan tightly and simmer until the chicken is very tender. This is an excellent way to cook tough chickens. Fowls which have been boiled may be cooked in this way, but of course young and tender chickens will have the finer flavor.

36

CORN MEAL WITH SAUSAGES

(Polenta con salsicce)

Cook in water one cup of yellow cornmeal making a stiff mush. Salt it well and when it is cooked spread out to cool on a bread board about half an inch thick. Then cut the mush into small squares.

Put in a saucepan several whole sausages with a little water, and when they are cooked skin and crush them and add some brown stock or tomato sauce.

Put the polenta (or cornmeal mush) in a fireproof receptacle, season with grated cheese, the crushed sausages and a piece of butter. Put it in the oven and serve when hot.

37

POLENTA PIE

(Polenta Pasticciata)

Make a very stiff mush of cornmeal cooked in milk. Salt it well and spread out on the bread board in a sheet about one inch thick. When cold, cut in little diamonds or squares and place these in a buttered baking dish. Prepare the **Bolognese souce** according to the following recipe: Chop ¼ lb. round steak, a slice of pork or bacon, one small carrot ¼ onion, one large piece celery. Put the meat and vegetables over the fire with a piece of butter. When the meat has browned add half a tablespoon of flour and wet the mixture with hot water or broth, allowing it to simmer from half an hour to an hour. It is done when it is the consistency of a thick gravy.

Make a smooth white sauce with milk cornstarch and butter. Over a layer of the polenta, cut as above and placed in the baking dish sprinkle some grated cheese and a few tablespoons each of the white sauce and the meat sauce. Repeat until the dish is full. Bake until the top is nicely browned. This dish seems very elaborate, but it is very delicious and a meal in itself.

The Bolognese sauce is also used to season macaroni or spaghetti in lieu of the tomato sauce or the brown stock.

38

STUFFED ROLLS

(Pagnottelle ripiene)

Take some rolls, and by means of a round opening on the top, as large as a half dollar piece or less, extract nearly all the crumb, leaving the crust intact, but not too thin. Wet inside and outside with hot milk, and when they are fairly soaked, dip in beaten eggs and fry them in lard or oil. When beginning to brown, fill them with meat that has been previously chopped and cooked. This chopped meat ought to be made with breast of chicken, chicken giblets, liver etc., brown stock and some flour to hold it together.

39

STEWED VEAL

(Stracotto di vitella)

The stock from this dish may very well be used to season macaroni or boiled rice. Care must be taken, however, not to draw away all the juice of the meat in order to have a sauce too rich at the expense of the principal dish.

Place in a saucepan one pound of veal or more, bone included, a piece of butter or some olive oil (or the two together) half a medium sized onion, one small carrot, two celery stalks cut in small pieces. Season with salt and pepper. Put it on a low fire, turn the meat over often and when browned add a pinch of flour and some tomato paste, bringing it to full cooking with water poured little by little. The flour is used to keep the sauce together and give it color, but care must be taken not to burn it, because in that case the sauce would have an unpleasant taste and a black, instead of a reddish color. The addition of dried mushrooms, previously softened in the water and slightly boiled in the sauce will add greatly to its taste.

As has been said the sauce can well be used to season spaghetti or risotto. The stewed veal can be served with some vegetable.

40

CHICKEN BONED AND STUFFED

(Pollo dissossato ripieno)

To remove the bones from a chicken the following instructions will be found useful.

Wash and singe the fowl: take off the head

and legs, and remove the tendons. When a fowl is to be boned it is not drawn. The work of boning is not difficult, but it requires practice. The skin must not be broken. Use a small pointed knife cut the skin down the full length of the back; then, beginning at the neck, carefully scrape the meat away from the bone, keeping the knife close to the bone. When the joints of the wings and legs are met, break them back and proceed to free the meat from the carcass. When one side is free, turn the fowl and do the same on the other side. The skin is drawn tightly over the breast-bone, and care must be used to detach it without piercing the skin. When the meat is free from the carcass, remove the bones from the legs and wings, turning the meat down or inside out, as the bones are exposed, and using care not to break the skin at the joints. The end bones of the wing cannot be removed, and the whole end joint may be cut off or left as it is.

Now that the fowl is boned make the following stuffing, regulating the quantity on the size of the chicken. Chop half a pound or more, of lean veal, and grind it afterwards, so that it may make a paste. Add a large piece of bread crumb soaked in broth, a tablespoon of grated cheese, three yolks of egg, salt, pepper and, if desired, just a taste of nutmeg. Finally mix also one or two slices of ham and tongue, cut in small pieces. Stuff the boned chicken with this filling, sew up the opening, wrap it tightly in a cloth and put to cook in water on a low fire. When taken from the water, remove the wrapping and brown it, first with butter, then in a sauce made in the following way: Break all the bones that have been extracted from the chicken, the head and neck included, and put them on the fire with dried meat cut in little pieces, butter, onion, celery and carrot, seasoned with salt and pepper. Make the sauce with the water in which the chicken has been boiled, which has naturally become a good chicken broth.

Before sending to the table, remove the thread with which the chicken has been sewed.

41

CHICKEN WITH TOMATOES

(Pollo alla contadina)

Take a young chicken and make some little holes in the skin in which you will put some sprigs of rosemary and a clove of garlic cut into five or six pieces. Put it on the fire with chopped lard and season with salt and pepper inside and outside. When it is well browned on all parts add tomatoes cut in pieces, taking care to remove previously all the seeds. Moisten with broth or water. Brown some potatoes in oil, fat or butter, previously cutting them into sections. When browned dip in the sauce of the chicken and serve the whole together.

42

CHICKEN WITH SHERRY

(Pollo al marsala)

Cut the chicken in big pieces and put it in the saucepan with one medium sized onion chopped fine and a piece of butter. Season with salt and pepper and, when it is well browned, add some broth and complete the cooking. Remove the excessive fat from the sauce by sifting through a sieve or otherwise, and put the chicken back on the fire with a glass of Sherry or Marsala wine, removing it from the fire as soon as the sauce begins to boil.

43

CHICKEN WITH SAUSAGES

(Pollo colle salsicce)

Chop fine half an onion and put it in a saucepan with a piece of butter and four or five slices of ham, half an inch wide. Over these ingredients place a whole chicken, season with pepper and a little salt and place on the fire. Brown it on all sides and, when the onion is all melted, add water or broth and three or four sausages freshly made. Let it cook on a low fire, seeing that the sauce remains liquid and does not dry up.

44

CHICKEN WITH EGG SAUCE

(Pollo in salsa d'uova)

Break into pieces a young chicken and put it in the saucepan with a piece of butter. Season with salt and pepper. When it is half browned sprinkle with a pinch of flour to give it color, then complete the cooking with broth. Remove it from the same and put it on a plate. Beat the yolk of one egg with the piece of half a lemon and pour it on the sauce of the chicken, allowing it to simmer for some minutes. Then pour on the chicken and serve hot.

45

CHICKEN BREASTS SAUTÈS

(Petti di pollo alla sautè)

Cut the breast of a fowl in very thin slices, give them the best possible shape and make a whole piece from the little pieces that will remain, cleaning well the breast-bone, crushing and mixing these. Season with salt and pepper and dip the slices in beaten eggs, leaving them for a few hours. Sprinkle with bread crumbs ground fine and sautè in butter. Serve with lemon.

If you want this dish more elaborate prepare a sauce in the following way: Put some good olive oil in a frying pan, just enough to cover the bottom, and cover the oil with a layer of dry mushrooms. Sprinkle over a small quantity of grated cheese and some bread crumbs. Repeat the same operation three or four times, according to the quantity, and finally season with olive oil, salt and pepper and small pieces of butter. Put the pan over the fire and when it has begun to boil pour a small cup of brown stock or broth and a little lemon juice. Remove the same from the fire and pour it on the chicken breast that have been browned as described above.

46

WILD DUCK

(Anitra selvatica)

Clean the duck, putting aside the giblets, and cut off the head and legs. Chop fine a thick slice of ham with both lean and fat together, with a moderate amount of celery, parsley, carrot and half medium sized onion. Put the chopped ham and vegetables in a saucepan and lay the duck on the whole, seasoning wtih salt and pepper. Brown on all sides and add water to complete the cooking.

Cabbage or lentils, cooked in water and afterward allowed to complete the cooking in the sauce obtained from the duck, form a good addition.

To remove the "gamey" taste from the wild duck, either wash it in vinegar before cooking or scald it in boiling water.

47

STEWED SQUABS

(Piccioni in umido)

Garnish the squabs with whole sage leaves and place them in a saucepan over a bed of small slices of ham containing both lean and fat, season with salt, pepper and olive oil. Place on the fire and when they begin to be browned, add a piece of butter and complete the cooking by pouring in some good broth. Before removing from the fire squeeze one lemon over them and garnish with squares or diamonds of toasted bread. Take care not to add too much salt on account of the ham and the broth both containing salt.

Note—Many of these dishes, it will be noticed, are made with broth. When meat broth is not available, it can be prepared with bouillon cubes or with Liebig or Armour Extracts. It is, however, always preferable to use broth made with fresh meat.

48

RAGOUT OF SQUABS

(Manicaretto di piccione)

Cut two or more squabs at the joints, preferably in four parts each, and put them on the fire with a slice of ham, a piece of butter, and a bunch of parsley. When they begin to dry, add some broth and — before they are completely cooked — their giblets and fresh mushrooms cut in slices. Continue pouring in broth and allow the whole to simmer on a low fire. Add another piece of butter over which some flour has been sprinkled, or flour alone. Before serving, remove the ham and the bunch of greens and squeeze some lemon juice over the squabs.

Some sweetbread may be added with good effect, but it must be first scalded and the skin removed.

49

SQUAB TIMBALE

(Timballo di piccioni)

Chop together some ham, onion, celery and carrot, add a piece of butter and place on the fire with one or two squabs, according to the number of guests. Add the giblets from the squabs and some more of chicken, if at hand. Season with salt and pepper, and when the pigeons are browned, pour over some broth to complete the cooking, taking care, however, that the sauce does not become too liquid. Remove the latter and place in it some macaroni that has been half cooked and drained. Keep the macaroni in the sauce on the fire, stirring them. Make a well reduced Bechamel sauce, then cut the squabs at the joints, removing the neck, the legs and the bones of the back, when you would not bone them entirely, which would be better. Cut the giblets in small pieces and remove the soft part of the onion.

When the macaroni have absorbed the sauce, season them with grated cheese, pieces of butter, diamonds or squares of ham, a taste of nutmeg and some truffles or dry mushrooms previously softened in water. Add finally the Bechamel sauce and mix the whole.

Take a sufficiently large mold, butter it and line it with soft pastry. Put everything in the mold, or timbale, cover it with the same pastry and put in the oven. Take out of the mold and serve hot. Three quarters of a pound of macaroni and two pigeons are enough for ten persons.

50
SALMI OF GAME
(Uccelli in salmi)

Roast the game completely, seasoning with salt and pepper. If the game be small birds, leave them whole, if big cut them in four parts. Remove all the heads and grind them together with some pieces of birds, or some whole little birds. Put in a saucepan one tablespoonful of butter one half pound of bacon or ham cut into dice, brown stock or broth, one tablespoonful each of chopped onion and carrot, one tablespoonful each of salt, thyme and sage.

Allow the sauce to simmer for half an hour then rub it through a sieve and place in it the roasted game. Make it boil until the cooking is completed and serve with toasted diamonds of bread.

51

STEWED HARE

(Stufato di lepre)

Take half of a good sized hare and, after cutting it in pieces, chop fine one medium sized onion, one clove of garlic, a stalk of celery and several leaves of rosemary. Put on the fire with some pieces of butter, two tablespoonfuls of olive oil and four or five strips of bacon or salt pork, when the whole has been browning for four or five minutes, put the pieces of hare inside the saucepan and season them with salt, pepper and spices. When it is browned, put a wineglass of white wine, some fresh mushrooms, or dry mushrooms previously softenend in water. Complete the cooking with broth and tomato sauce and, if necessary, add another piece of butter.

52

STEWED RABBIT

(Coniglio in umido)

After washing the rabbit, cut it in rather large pieces and put it on the fire to drive away the water that is to be drained. When quite dry, put in the saucepan a piece of butter, a little oil, and a hash composed of the liver of the rabbit itself, a small piece of corned beef and some onion, celery, carrot and parsley. Season with salt and pepper. Stir often and when it is browned add some tomato sauce and another piece of butter.

53

GREEN SAUCE

(Salsa verde)

Chop all together some capers that have been in vinegar, one anchovy, a small slice of onion and just a taste of garlic. Crush the resulting hash with the blade of a knife to make it very fine. Add a sprig of parsley, chopped together with some leaves of basil and dissolve the whole in very good olive oil and lemon juice.

This sauce is excellent to season boiled chicken or cold boiled fish or hard boiled eggs.

Green Peppers can take the place of capers, if these are not at hand.

54

WHITE SAUCE

(Salsa bianca)

This sauce can be served with boiled asparagus or with cauliflower. The ingredients are ¼ lb. of butter, a tablespoonful of flour, a tablespoonful vinegar, one yolk of egg, salt and pepper, broth or water in sufficient quantity.

Put first on the fire the flour with half the butter and when it begins to be browned pour over it the broth or the water little by little, stirring with the wooden spoon and adding the rest of the butter and the vinegar without making the water boil too much. When taken off the fire add the yolk of the egg, stir and serve.

55

YELLOW SAUCE

(Salsa gialla)

This sauce is especially good for boiled fish, and the quantities indicated below are sufficient for a piece of fish or a whole fish weighing about a pound.

Put on the fire in a little saucepan one teaspoonful of flour and two ounces of butter, and when the flour begins to be browned, pour over it little by little one cup of the broth of the fish, that is to say of the water in which the fish has been boiled. When you see that the flour does not rise in the boiling water, take away the sauce from the flour and pour over two tablespoonfuls of olive oil and the yolk of an egg, stirring and mixing everything well. Squeeze in the sauce half a lemon and season generously with salt and pepper. Let it cool and then pour over the fish that is to be served with a sprig of parsley.

This sauce must have the appearance of a cream and must not be too liquid, in order that it may remain attached to the fish.

56

SAUCE FOR BROILED FISH

(Salsa per pesce in gratella)

This sauce is composed of yolks of eggs, salted anchovies, olive oil and lemon juice. Boil the eggs in their shell for ten minutes and for every hard yolk take one large anchovy or two small. Bone the anchovies and rub them on the sieve together with the hard (or semi-hard) yolks, and dissolve all with oil and lemon juice to reduce it like a cream. Cover with this sauce the broiled fish before sending to the table, or serve aside in a gravy boat.

57

CAPER SAUCE

(Salsa con capperi)

This sauce is especially adapted for boiled fish and the quantities are for a little more than one pound of fish. The ingredients are two ounces of butter, two ounces of capers soaked in vinegar one teaspoonful of flour, salt, pepper and vinegar.

Boil the fish and, when it is left warm in its broth, prepare the sauce. Put on the fire the flour with half of the butter, mix it and when it begins to take color, add the remaining butter.

Let boil a little and then pour one half cup of the broth of the fish: season generously with salt and pepper and take the saucepan from the fire. Then throw in it the capers, half whole, half chopped, and some drops of vinegar, but taste it to dose the sauce so that it is pleasant to the taste and as thick as liquid cream.

It is well to observe here that these sauces in which butter is used together with acids, such as vinegar, are not for weak stomachs and should be partaken of sparingly.

58
GENOVESE SAUCE
(Salsa genovese)

Chop fine a sprig of parsley and half a clove of garlic. Then mix with some capers soaked in vinegar, one anchovy, one hard yolk of egg, three pitless olives, a crumb of bread as big as an egg, soaked in vinegar. Grind all these ingredients, rub through a sieve and dissolve in olive oil, dosing right by tasting.

59
BALSAMELLA SAUCE
(Salsa balsamella)

This sauce resembles the famous French Bèchamel Sauce, but it is simpler in its composition.

Put in a saucepan one tablespoonful of flour and a piece of butter as big as an egg. Stir the flour and the butter together while keeping them over the fire. When the flour begins to be browned, pour over a pint of milk, continually stirring with a wooden spoon until you see the liquid condensed like a cream. This is the **Balsamella.** If it is too thick add some milk, if too liquid put back on the fire with another piece of butter dipped in flour.

A good **Balsamella** and some well prepared brown stock are the base and the principal secret of many savory dishes.

60

CURLED OMELET

(Frittata in riccioli)

Boil a bunch of spinach and rub it through a sieve. Beat two eggs, season with salt and pepper and mix with them enough spinach to make the eggs appear green. Put the frying pan on the fire with only enough oil to grease it and when very hot put in a portion of the eggs, moving the frying pan so as to make a very thin omelet. When well cooked, remove it from the frying pan and repeat the operation once or twice in order to have two or three very thin omelets. Put these one over the other and cut them in small strips that are to be browned in butter adding a little grated cheese. These strips of omelet, resembling noodles, form a tasty and attractive dressing for a fricandeau (veal stew) or a similar dish.

61

VEAL KIDNEY OMELET

(Frittata di rognone di vitella)

Take a veal kidney, open it lengthwise and leave all its fat. Season with oil, salt and pepper, broil it and cut in thin slices. Beat enough eggs in proportion to the size of the kidney, season them with salt and pepper, both in moderate quantity and mix with them a sprig of parsley and some grated cheese. Put the sliced kidney in the eggs, mix all together and make an omelet with some butter.

62

PUFF PASTE

(Pasta sfoglia)

The **Pasta sfoglia** is not too difficult to make and if the following instructions are carefully followed, this fine and light paste can easily be prepared. It is well to have a marble slab to roll it on but this is not absolutely necessary. A warm, damp day is not favorable for the making of the **Pasta sfoglia,** which succeeds better when the weather is cold and dry.

Mix half a pound of flour of the very best quality with a piece of butter as big as a walnut, some warm, but not hot water, enough salt and a teaspoonful of good brandy. When the paste is formed knead it well for about half an hour, first with the hands, then throwing it repeatedly with force against the bread board. Make a cake of a rectangular form, wrap it in cloth and let it rest for a while. Meanwhile work with the hand ½ lb. of butter that has been kept previously on ice or, better, in a bowl of ice-water, until it becomes smooth and flexible, then make of it a little cake like that of the paste and throw it in a bowl of cold water. When the dough has rested take the butter from the water, wipe it with a cloth and dip it in flour.

Roll the paste only as long as it is necessary to enclose within the cake of butter. This is placed in the middle and the edges of the sheet of paste are drawn over it, closing well with fingers moistened in a little water so that no air remains inside. Then begin to flatten, first with the hands, then with the rolling pin, making the sheet as thin as possible, but taking care that the butter does not come out. If this happens throw at once a little flour where the butter appears and always have the marble slab (or bread board) and the rolling pin sprinkled with flour. Fold it over, making three even layers of paste, and again roll the folded strip, repeating the operation six times and letting the paste rest from time to time for a few minutes. At the last time, fold it in two and reduce it to the necessary thickness that is, about one third of an inch. After each folding press the edges gently with the rolling pin to shut in the air, and turn the paste so as to roll in a different direction.

When the paste has had six turns cut it into the desired forms and put on ice, or in a cold place for twenty to thirty minutes before putting it on the oven, which must be very hot, with the greatest heat at the bottom.

The puff past is used for patè shells and vol-au-vent cake and for light pastries of all kinds.

63

PASTE FOR FRYING

(Pastella per fritto)

Dilute three teaspoonfuls of flour with two teaspoonfuls of oil. Add two eggs, a pinch of salt, and mix well. This mixture will take on the aspect of a smooth cream and is used to glaze fried brains, sweetbreads and the like. All these things are first to be scalded in boiling salt water. Add a pinch of salt and one of pepper when taking from the water. The brains, sweetbreads etc. are then to be cut in irregular pieces, thrown into the paste, or cream, described above and fried in oil or good lard.

In frying these are often united to liver or veal cutlets. The liver must be cut in very thin slices and the cutlets beaten with the side of a big knife and given a good shape. Season with salt and pepper, dip in beaten egg and after a few hours sprinkle with bread crumbs and fry. Serve with lemon.

64

CHICKEN STUFFING

(Ripieno di pollo)

The ingredients are ¼ lb. lean veal or pork or breast of turkey and chicken giblets. Cook this meat together with a little hash of onion, parsley, celery, carrot and butter. Season with salt pepper and spices, moistening it with broth. Take dry from the fire, take off the soft parts of the giblets, add a few dry mushrooms soft ened in water, a little slice of lean fat ham and chop everything fine. Into the sauce that has remained from the cooking throw enough bread-crumbs to make a tablespoonful of hard soaked bread. Mix it with the chopped hash, add a pinch of grated cheese and two eggs and fill the chicken with all this, sewing up the opening afterwards. The chicken can be boiled or stewed. If boiled you will have an excellent bouillon, but pay attention when cutting the chicken to extract the stuffing in one piece in order to slice it.

65

MEAT STUFFING FOR VOL-AU-VENT

(Ripieno di carne per pasticcini di pasta sfoglia)

This stuffing can be made either with stewed veal or chicken giblets or sweetbreads. The latter are preferable, being more delicate and a taste of truffles greatly improves the stuffing. If sweetbreads are used, put them on the fire with a piece of butter and season with salt and pepper. When they have begun to take color, complete the cooking with some brown stock, then cut them in pieces as little as a bean. Add one or two spoons of **Balsamella** (see No. 54) a little tongue, one or two slices of ham cut in little squares, a pinch of grated cheese and a taste of nutmeg, seeing that the ingredients are in such quantities as to make the mixture tasty and delicate. Leave it cool well, as in this way it hardens and can be worked better.

In order to enclose it in patè shells made with puff-paste (see No. 57) there are two ways. One is to cook the shells filled with the stuffing, the other to fill them after they are cooked. In the first case put the stuffing in the prepared disk of paste, moisten the edge with a wet finger, cover with another disk of paste and cook. In the second case, which is more convenient because the shells can be prepared one day before, the two disks are put together without the stuffing, but in the upper disk a circular cut must be made as large as a half dollar coin. The pàtè on cooking swells and leaves an empty space in the interior. Lifting with the point of a knife the little circle above, which has the form of a cover, the interior space can be made larger, filled with the stuffing and covered with the little cover. In this way it is enough to warm them before sending to the table. The puff-paste must always be glazed with the yolk of eggs.

If a large vol-au-vent is to be filled instead of little patè-shells, a ragout of chicken giblets and sweetbread, cut in large pieces, is better.

66
PORK LIVER FRIED
(Fegato di maiale fritto)

Cut in to thin slices some pork liver, sprinkle with flour and fry in good lard. It must be served with its sauce. Squeeze in a lemon while it is frying.

67
FRIED CROQUETTES, BOLOGNA STYLE
(Fritto composto alla Bolognese)

Take a piece of stewed lean veal, a little brain boiled or stewed, and a slice of ham. Chop and grind everything fine. Add a yolk of egg or a whole egg, according to the quantity, and a little **Balsamella** (see No. 54). Put the hash on the fire and stir until the egg is cooked. Add finally grated cheese, a taste of nutmeg, and, if you have them, some truffles chopped very fine and put in a plate. When quite cold make some little balls as large as a walnut and roll them in flour. Then dip in beaten egg and bread crumb ground very fine, repeating the operation twice, and fry.

68

ROMAN FRY

(Fritto alla Romana)

I.

Put on the fire a hash of onion and butter and when it is well browned cook in it a piece of lean veal seasoned with salt and pepper. When the meat begins to brown put in a little sherry wine to complete the cooking.

Pound the whole to soften it a little using the sauce remained and if this is not enough add some broth and finally the yolk of an egg. See that the whole is not softened too much.

Now take some wafers, not too thin and cut them in squares similar to those used by druggists. Beat one egg and the white from the other egg, then take a wafer, dip it in the egg and place it on a layer of bread crumbs ground fine. On the wafer put a little ball of the compound above, then dip another wafer in the egg, make it touch the bread crumbs only from the part that remains outside, and with this cover the compound attaching it to the lower wafer. Sprinkle again with bread crumbs if necessary and put the piece aside repeating the operation until all the meat is disposed of. Cook in oil or fat and serve with lemon.

With half a pound of meat about twenty filled wafers should be obtained.

69
ROMAN FRY
II.

This can be made when you happen to have some breast of roast chicken left over. Some chicken breast, two or three slices of tongue and ham, one tablespoonful of grated cheese, a taste of nutmeg, are the ingredients used. Remove the skin of the chicken and cut it as well as the tongue and the ham, into little cubes. Make a **Balsamella** (see No. 54) in sufficient quantity and when it is cooked add the above ingredients and let it cool well to fry using the wafer as in the preceding.

70
RICE PANCAKE
(Frittelle di riso)

Cook thoroughly ¼ lb. of rice in about a pint of water giving it taste with a little piece of sugar and a taste of lemon peel. Leave it cool and then add three yolks of eggs and a little flour. Mix well and let the whole rest for several hours. When you are going to fry beat the white of an egg to a froth, add it to the rice and throw into the frying pan one tablespoonful at a time.

Serve hot sprinkled with confectionery sugar.

71

KIDNEY SAUTE'

(Rognoni saltati)

Take one large kidney, or two or three small kidneys, open them and remove all the fat. Cut lengthwise in thin slices, salt and pour as much boiling water as is needed to cover them. When the water is thoroughly cooled, drain it and wipe well the slices with a cloth, then put them in a frying pan with a small piece of butter. Turn them often and when they have cooked for five minutes put in a pinch of flour and season with salt and pepper. Leave them on the fire until thoroughly cooked and when you are going to take them away add another piece of butter, a sprig of chopped parsley and a little broth if needed. The kidney must not be kept too much on the fire, because in that case it hardens.

72

LEG OF MUTTON IN CASSEROLE

(Cosciotto di castrato in cazzaruola)

Take a shoulder or a leg of mutton and after having boned, it lard it with small pieces of bacon dipped in salt and pepper. Salt moderately the meat then tie it tight and put it on the fire in a pan that contains a piece of butter and one large onion larded with clover. When it begins to brown, take it away from the fire and add a cup of broth, or of water, a little bunch of greens and some tomatoes cut in pieces. Put again on a low fire and let it simmer for three hours, keeping the saucepan closed, but opening from time to time to turn the meat. When it is cooked, throw away the onion, rub the sauce through a sieve, remove its fat and put it with the meat when served. The mutton must not be overdone, for in this case it cannot be sliced.

73

STEWED CUTLETS

(Scaloppine alla Livornese)

Take some slices of tender beef, beat them well and put them in a saucepan with a piece of butter. When this is all melted, put one or two table-spoonfuls of broth to complete the cooking, season with salt and pepper, add a pinch of flour and before taking them from the fire put in a pinch of chopped parsley.

74

CUTLETS OF CHOPPED MEAT

(Scaloppine di carne battuta)

Take some good lean beef, clean it well, removing all little skins and tendons, then first chop and after grind the meat fine in the grinder. Season with salt, pepper and a pinch of grated cheese. Mix well and give the meat the form of a ball then with bread crumbs over and beneath flatten it with the rolling pin on the bread board making a sheet of meat as thick as a silver dollar. Cut it in square pieces, as large as the palm of the hand and cook in a saucepan with butter. When these cutlets are browned, pour over some tomato sauce and serve.

If you prefer, use your hands instead of the rolling pin and then you can give them the shapes you like.

If you have some left over meat this can perfectly well be mixed with the raw meat and chopped and ground together.

75

VEAL CUTLETS STEWED

(Scaloppine alla Genovese)

Cut some lean veal meat into slices and, supposing it be a pound or a little more, without bones, chop one fourth of a middle-sized onion and put it in a saucepan with oil and a little piece of butter. Put over the cutlets, one layer over the other, season with salt and butter and put on the fire. When the meat which is below is browned put in a teaspoonful of flour and after a while a hash of parsley with half a clove of garlic. Then detach the cutlets the one from the other, mix them, let them drink in the sauce, then pour hot water and a little tomato sauce. Make it boil slowly and not much to complete the cooking and serve with abundant sauce and with little diamonds of toast.

76
STUFFED CUTLET
(Braciuoline ripiene)

Slice from a piece of veal (about one pound) seven or eight cutlets and beat them well with a knife blade to flatten them. Then chop some tender veal meat and one or two slices of ham and add a small quantity of marrow bone (of veal) and grated cheese. The marrow and the grated cheese must be reduced to a paste with the blade of a knife. One egg is then added to tie up the hash and a pinch of pepper, but no salt on account of the ham and the cheese that already contain it. Spread the cutlets and put the hash in the middle, then roll them up and tie them with strong thread.

Now prepare a small hash with a little onion, a piece of celery a piece of carrot and a small quantity of corned beef and put it in the fire in a saucepan with a small piece of butter, at the same time that you put the cutlets. Season with salt and pepper and when they begin to brown pour some tomato sauce and complete the cooking with water. Before serving, remove the thread with which the cutlets have been tied.

77

MEAT OMELETTE
(Polpettone)

Take one pound of veal, without bones, clean it well taking away all skins and tendons and then chop it together with a slice of ham. Season moderately with salt pepper and spices, add one whole egg then with moistened hands make a ball of the chopped meat and sprinkle with flour.

Make a hash with two or three slices of onion (not more) parsley, celery, and carrot, put it on the fire with a piece of butter and when it is browned throw in the **Polpettone.** Brown well on all sides and then pour in the saucepan half a tumbler of water in which half a tablespoonful of flour has been previously diluted. Cover and make it simmer on a very low fire, seeing that it doesn't burn. When you serve with the gravy squeeze the juice of half a lemon over it.

If desired a hard boiled egg can be put shelled in the center of the meat ball, so that it gives it a better appearance when sliced.

78

LAMB WITH PEAS

(Agnello ai piselli)

Take a piece of lamb from the hind side, lard it with two cloves of garlic cut in little strips and with some sprigs of rosemary. Chop fine a piece of lard and a slice of corned beef. Put the lamb on the fire with this hash and a little oil and let it brown after seasoning with salt and pepper. When it is browned add a piece of butter, some tomato sauce, or tomato paste dissolved in water or soup stock and complete the cooking. Take away the lamb, put the peas in the gravy, and when they have simmered a little and are cooked put back the lamb and serve.

79

SHOULDER OF LAMB

(Spalla d'agnello)

Cut the meat of a shoulder of lamb in small pieces, or squares. Chop two small onions, brown them with a piece of butter and when they are browned put the meat and season with salt and pepper. Wait until the meat begins to brown and then add another piece of butter dipped in flour. Mix the whole and complete the cooking with soup stock or water with bouillon cubes poured in little by little.

80

BREAST OF VEAL STEWED

(Stufatino di petto di vitella)

Break a piece of breast of veal leaving all its bones.

Make a hash with garlic, parsley, celery and carrot; add oil, pepper and salt and put on the fire with the meat. Turn it over often, and when it begins to brown, sprinkle over a pinch of flour and a little tomato sauce or tomato paste diluted in water.. Complete the cooking with broth or water. Finally add a piece of butter and pieces of celery cut in big pieces which must have been before half cooked in water and browned in butter. Care must be taken to keep the saucepan always covered, in this as in other stews.

81

VEAL WITH GRAVY

(Vitella in guazzetto)

First take about one pound of veal and tie it well. Then cover the bottom of the saucepan with some thin slices of corned beef and a piece of butter. Over this place half a lemon cut in four thin slices from which the skin and the seeds must be removed. Over all this put the veal which must be well browned on all sides, but care must be taken not to burn it on account of the small quantity of liquid. Afterward, remove the superfluous fat and pour over a cup of hot milk, that has boiled. Cover the saucepan and complete the cooking. Before serving rub the gravy through a sieve.

82

TRIPE WITH GRAVY

Boil some tripe in water and when it is boiled, cut it in strips, one quarter of an inch wide and wipe it well with a cloth. Then put it in a saucepan with butter, and when this is melted, add some brown stock or good tomato sauce. Season with salt and pepper, cook thoroughly and add a pinch of grated cheese before taking from the saucepan.

83

VEAL LIVER IN GRAVY

(Fegato di vitella al sugo)

Chop fine a scallion or an onion, make it brown in oil and butter, and when it has taken a dark red color, throw in the liver cut in thin slices. When half cooked season with salt, pepper and a pinch of chopped parsley. Make it simmer on a low fire so that the gravy remains, and serve in its gravy, squeezing over some lemon juice when sent to the table.

In this and in similar cases, when using scallions or onions, some advise putting these in a cloth after being chopped and dip them in cold water squeezing them dry after.

84

MUTTON CUTLETS AND FILET OF VEAL

(Braciuole di castrato e filetto di vitella)

Put in saucepan a slice of ham, some butter, a little bunch composed of carrot, celery and stems of parsley and over this some whole cutlets of mutton seasoned with salt and pepper. Make them brown on both sides, add another piece of butter, if necessary, and add to the cutlets some chicken giblets, sweetbreads and fresh or dry mushrooms (the latter softened in water, all cut in pieces. When all this begins to brown, pour some soup stock and let it simmer on a low fire. Sprinkle a little flour and finally pour a wineglass (or half a tumbler) of white wine leaving it boil a little more. When ready to serve remove the ham and the greens, rub the gray through a sieve and remove the superfluous fat.

85

TENDERLOIN WITH MARSALA

(Filetto al marsala)

Roll a piece of the tenderloin, tie it and, if it is about two pounds, put it on the fire with a middle-sized onion cut in thin slices, some thin slices of ham and a piece of butter, seasoning but moderately with salt and pepper. When it is browned from all sides and the onion is consumed, sprinkle a pinch of flour, let this take color and then pour some soup stock or water. Make it simmer on a low fire, then rub the gravy through a sieve, skim off the fat and with this and half a small tumbler of Marsala or Sherry wine put it back on the fire to simmer again. Serve with the gravy neither too liquid nor too thick.

The filet can also be larded with bacon and cooked in butter and Marsala only.

86

MEAT GENOVESE

(Carne alla Genovese)

Take thick slices of good lean veal, weighing about a pound, beat it and flatten it well. Beat three or four eggs, season them with salt and pepper, a pinch of grated cheese and some chopped parsley. Fry the eggs in butter in the form of an omelet about the size of the meat over which it will be laid, cutting it where it overlaps and putting the pieces where it lacks so as to cover the meat entirely. After that roll tight the meat together with the omelet and tie it with thread. Then sprinkle some flour over it and put it in a saucepan with a piece of butter, seasoning with salt and pepper. When it is well browned on all sides, pour some soup stock to complete the cooking and serve it in its gravy which will be thick enough on account of the gravy.

87

RICE PUDDING WITH GIBLETS

(Sfornato di riso con rigoglie)

Make a good brown stock (see No. 13) and use the same for the rice as well as for the giblets. To these add some thin slices of ham and brown them first in butter, seasoned moderately with salt and pepper, completing the cooking with brown stock. A taste of mushrooms will be found useful.

Brown the rice equally in butter, then complete the cooking with hot water. Drain and put the brown stock, adding grated cheese and two beaten eggs, when the rice has cooled a little.

Take a smooth mold, round or oval, grease it evenly with butter, cover the bottom with buttered paper and place in it the rice to harden it in the oven. When taken from the mold pour over the gravy from the giblets, slighthly thickened with a pinch of flour and serve with the giblets around, seeing that there is plenty of gravy for them.

88

PUDDING GENOESE

(Budino alla genovese)

Chop together a slice of veal, some chicken breast and two slices of ham and then grind or better pound them, with a small piece of butter, a tablespoonful of grated cheese and a crumb of bread soaked with milk. Rub through a sieve and add three tablespoonfuls of **Balsamella** (see No. 54) which you will make thick enough for this dish, three eggs and just a taste of nutmeg, mixing everything well.

Take a smooth mold, grease it evenly with butter and put on the bottom a sheet of paper, cut according to the shape of the bottom and equally greased with butter. Pour over the above ingredients and cook in a vessel immersed in boiling water (double boiler).

When taken from the mold, remove the paper and in its place put a gravy formed with chopped chicken giblets cooked in brown stock. Serve hot.

89

LIVER LOAF

(Pane di fegato)

Cut about one pound of veal liver in thin slices and four chicken livers in two parts and put all this in a saucepan with rosemary and a piece of butter. When this is melted put in another piece and season with salt and pepper. After four or five minutes at a live fire, remove the liver (dry) and grind it together with the rosemary. In the gravy that remains in the saucepan put a big crumb of bread, cut into small pieces and make a paste that will also be ground with the liver. Then rub everything through a sieve, add one whole egg and two yolks and a pinch of grated cheese, diluting with brown stock or water. Finally put in a smooth mold with a sheet of paper in the bottom, all evenly greased with butter and cook in a double boiler. Remove from the mold when cool and serve cold, with gelatine.

90

VEAL WITH TUNNY

(Vitello tonnato)

Take two pounds of meat without bones, remove the fat and tendons, then lard it with two anchovies. These must be washed and boned and cut lengthwise, after opening them, making in all eight pieces. Tie the piece of meat not very tight and boil it for an hour and a half in enough water to cover it completely. Previously put into the water one quarter of an onion larded with clover, one leaf of laurel, celery, carrot and parsley. Salt the water generously and don't put the veal in until it is boiling. When the veal is cooked, untie, dry it and keep it for two or three days in the following sauce in quantity sufficient to cover it.

Grind ¼ pound tunny fish preserved in olive oil and two anchovies, crush them well with the blade of a knife and rub through a sieve adding good olive oil in abundance little by little, and squeeze in one whole lemon, so that the sauce should remain liquid. Finally mix in some capers soaked in vinegar.

Serve the veal cold, in thin slices, with the sauce.

The stock of the veal can be rubbed through a sieve and used for risotto.

91

STUFFED ITALIAN SQUASH

(Zucchini ripieni)

For a description of the **Zucchini** see No. 32.

To make the stuffed zucchini first cut them lengthwise in two halves and remove the interior pulp, leaving space enough for the filling.

Take some lean veal (quantity in proportion to the squashes) cut it into pieces and place it on the fire in a saucepan with a hash of onion, parsley, celery, carrot, a little corned beef cut in little pieces, a little oil, salt and pepper. Stir it often with a spoon and when the meat is brown pour in a cup of water and then another after a while. Then rub the gravy through a sieve and put it aside.

Chop the cooked meat fine and grind it in the grinder and make a hash of it and one egg, a little grated cheese, a crumb of bread boiled in milk or in soup stock and just a taste of nutmeg. Put this hash inside each half squash and put them to brown in butter, completing the cooking with the gravy set aside.

92

STRING BEANS AND SQUASHES SAUTE'

(Fagiolini e zucchini sautè)

Brown in butter some string beans, that have been previously half cooked in water and some raw squashes cut in cubes. Put the squashes in only when the butter is beginning to brown. Season moderately with salt and butter and add some brown stock or good tomato sauce.

93

STRING BEANS WITH EGG SAUCE

(Fagiuolini in salsa d'uovo)

Take less than a pound of string beans, cutting off the two points and removing all the strings, and then cook them partially in water moderately salted. Take them from the kettle, drain, and brown with butter, salt and pepper. Beat one yolk with a teaspoonful of flour and the juice of half a small lemon, dilute with half a cup of cold broth from which the fat has been removed and put this liquid on the fire in a small saucepan stirring continually. When the liquid has become, through the cooking, like a cream, pour it on the string beans that you will keep on the fire a little longer, with the sauce. The string beans so prepared can be served with boiled beef.

94

STRING BEANS IN MOLD

(Sformato di fagiolini)

Take one pound of string beans, seeing that they are quite tender. Cut off the ends and remove the strings. Throw them into boiling water with a pinch of salt and when they are half cooked take them away and put them in cold water. If you have brown stock complete the cooking with this and with butter, otherwise brown a piece of onion, some parsley, a piece of celery and olive oil. When the onion is browned put in the string beans and complete the cooking with a little water if necessary.

Prepare a **Balsamella** sauce (No. 54) with a small piece of butter, half a teaspoonful of flour and half a cup of milk. With this, a tablespoonful of grated cheese and four beaten eggs bind the string beans when they are cold, mix and put in a mold, evenly greased with butter and the bottom covered with paper. Cook in a double boiler and serve hot.

95

CAULIFLOWER IN MOLD

(Sformato di cavolfiore)

Take a good sized cauliflower, remove the stalk and outside leaves, half cook it in water and then cut it into small pieces. Salt them and put them to brown with a little piece of butter and then complete the cooking with a cup of milk. Then rub them through a sieve. Prepare a **Balsamella** (No. 54) and add it to the cauliflower with 3 beaten eggs and a tablespoonful of grated cheese.

Cook in a greased mold and serve hot.

96

ARTICHOKES IN MOLD

(Sformato di carciofi)

Remove the outside leaves of the artichokes, the harder part of all leaves, and clean the stalks without removing them.

Cut each artichoke into four parts and put them to boil in salt water for only five minutes. If left longer on the fire they become too soaked in water and lose their taste. Remove from the water, drain them, grind or pound and rub them through a sieve. Season the pulp so obtained with two or three beaten eggs, two or three tablespoonfuls of **Balsamella** (No. 54) grated cheese, salt and a taste of nutmeg, but taste the seasoning several times to see that it is correctly dosed.

Place in a mold with brown stock or meat gravy (in that case use a mold with a hole) and cook in double boiler.

97

FRIED MUSHROOMS

(Funghi fritti)

Choose middle-sized mushrooms, which are also of the right ripeness: when they are too big they are too soft and if small they are too hard.

Scrape the stems, wash them carefully but do not keep in water, for then they would lose their pleasant odor. Then cut them in rather large slices and dip them in flour before putting in the frying pan. Olive oil is best for frying mushrooms and the seasoning is composed exclusively of salt and pepper to be applied when they are frying. They can also be dipped in beaten eggs after being sprinkled with flour, but this is superfluous.

98

STEWED MUSHROOMS
(Funghi in umido)

For a stew the mushrooms ought to be below middle-size. Clean, wash and cut as for the preceding. Put a saucepan on the fire with olive oil, one or two cloves of oil and some mint leaves. When the oil begins to splutter, put the mushrooms in without dipping in flour, season with salt and pepper and when they are half cooked pour in some tomato sauce. Be sparing however, with the seasoning, in order that the mushrooms do not absorb it too much and so lose some of their own delicate flavor.

99

DRIED MUSHROOMS
(Funghi secchi)

Mushrooms are an excellent condiment of various dishes and for this reason it is well to have some always at hand. Since, however, it is not always possible to have them fresh, the following recipe to prepare dried mushrooms will be found useful.

First of all wait until there is a sunny day Choose young mushrooms middle sized or big, but not too soft. Scrape the stem, clean them well in order to remove the earth and, without washing cut them in big pieces. This because when dried they diminish considerably in size. Keep these pieces exposed in the sun for two or three days, then thread them on a string (practising a hole in them) and keep in a well ventilated room or in the sun until they become quite dry. Then put them away well closed in a paper bag, but don't fail to look at them from time to time to see if it is necessary to expose them some more to sun and ventilation.

To use them soften in warm water, but keep them in as little as possible, so that they do not lose their delicate flavor. The best time to dry the mushrooms is June or July.

100

FRIED EGG-PLANTS

(Melanzane fritte)

Egg-plant or, as they are also called, mad-apples are an excellent vegetable which may be used as dressing or as a dish by itself. Small or middle-sized egg-plants are to be preferred, as the big ones have sometimes a slightly bitter taste.

Remove the skin, cut into cubes, salt and leave them in a plate for a few hours. Then wipe them to remove the juice that they have thrown out, dip in flour and fry in oil.

101

STEWED EGG-PLANTS

(Melanzane in umido)

Remove the skin, cut them into cubes and place on the fire with a piece of butter. When this is all absorbed, complete the cooking with tomato sauce (No. 12).

102

EGG-PLANTS IN THE OVEN

(Melanzane al forno)

Skin five or six egg-plants, cut them in round slices and salt them so that they throw out the water that they contain. After a few hours dip in flour and frying oil.

Take a fireproof vase or baking tin and place the slices in layers, with grated cheese between each layer, abundantly seasoned with tomato sauce (No. 12).

Beat one egg with a pinch of salt, a tablespoonful of tomato sauce, a teaspoonful of grated cheese and two of crumbs of bread, and cover the upper layer with this sauce. Put the vase in the oven and when the egg is coagulated, serve hot.

103

DRESSING OF CELERY

(Sedano per contorno)

The following are three ways to prepare celery to be served as seasoning or seasoning for meat dishes. For the first two make the pieces about four inches long, and two inches for the third. The stalk must be skinned, cut crosswise and left attached to the rib of the celery. Boil it in water moderately salted not over five minutes and remove dry.

1. Put the celery to brown in butter, then complete the cooking with brown stock (No. 13) and sprinkle with grated cheese when serving.

2. Put in saucepan a piece of butter and a hash made with ham and a middle sized onion, chopped fine. Add two cloves and make it boil. When the onion is browned add soup stock or hot water with bouillon cubes and complete the cooking. Then rub everything through a sieve and put the gravy in a plate with the celery, seasoning with pepper only, as the salt is already in the ham and serve with the gravy.

3. Dip the celery in flour and in the paste for frying (No. 58) and fry in fat or oil. Or else

dip in flour and then in beaten egg, wrap in bread crumbs and fry.

104

ARTICHOKES WITH SAUCE

(Carciofi in salsa)

Remove the hard leaves of the artichokes, cut the points and skin the stalk. Divide each artichoke into four parts or six if they are big, and put them on the fire with butter in proportion, seasoning with salt and pepper. Shake the saucepan to turn them and when they have absorbed a good part of the melted butter, pour in some broth to complete the cooking. Remove them dry, and in the gravy that remains put a pinch of chopped parsley, one or two teaspoonfuls of cheese grated fine, lemon juice, more salt and pepper if needed, and, mixing the whole, make it simmer for a while. Then remove the sauce from the fire and add one or two yolks of egg, according to the quantity and put back on the fire with more broth to make the sauce loose. Put the artichokes in the sauce this second time to heat them and serve especially as a side-dish for boiled meat.

105

STUFFED ARTICHOKES

(Carciofi ripieni)

Cut the stalk at the base, remove the small outside leaves and wash the artichokes. Then cut the top and open the internal leaves so that you can cut the bottom with a small knife and remove the hairy part if it is there. Keep aside the small interior leaves to put them with the stuffing. This, if to be used, for example, for six artichokes, must be composed of the above small leaves, ⅛ lb. of ham more lean than fat, one fourth of a small onion, just a taste of garlic, some leaves of celery or parsley, a pinch of dry mushrooms, softened in water, a crumb of bread and a pinch of pepper, but no salt.

First chop the ham, then grind everything together and with the hash fill the artichokes, and put them to cook standing on their stalks in a saucepan with some oil, salt and pepper. Some prefer to give the artichokes a half cooking in water before stuffing it, but it is hardly advisable, because in this way they lose part of their special flavor.

106

ARTICHOKES STUFFED WITH MEAT

(Carciofi ripieni di carne)

For six artichokes, make the following stuffing:

¼ lb. lean veal.
Two slices of ham, more fat than lean.
The interior part of the artichokes.
One fourth of onion (small).

Some leaves of parsley.
One pinch of softened dried mushrooms.
One small crumb of bread rolled and sifted.
One pinch of grated cheese.

When the artichokes have been browned with oil alone, pour a little water and cover with a moistened cloth kept in place by the cover. The steam that surrounds the artichokes cooks them better.

107

PEAS WITH ONION SAUCE

(Piselli alla francese)

The following recipe is good for one of fresh peas. Take two young onions, cut them in half, put some stems of parsley in the middle and tie them. Then put them into the fire with a piece of butter and when they are browned, pour over a cup of soup stock. Make it boil and when the onions are softened rub them through a sieve together with the gravy that you will then put on the fire with the peas and two whole hearts of lettuce. Season with salt and pepper and let it simmer. When the peas are half cooked add another piece of butter dipped in a scant tablespoonful of flour and pour in some broth, if necessary. Before sending to the table put in two yolks of eggs dissolved in a little broth.

II

The following recipe is simpler than the preceding, but not so delicate. Cut an onion in very thin slices and put it on the fire in a saucepan with a little butter. When it is well browned add a pinch of flour, mix and then add according to the quantity, a cup or two of soup stock or water with bouillon cubes and allow the flour to cook. Put in the peas, season with salt and pepper and add, when they are half cooked, one or two whole hearts of lettuce. Let it simmer, seeing that the gravy is not too thick.

Before serving remove the lettuce.

108

PEAS WITH HAM

(Piselli col prosciutto)

Cut in two one or two young onions, according to the quantity of the peas and put them on the fire with oil and one thick slice of ham cut into small cubes. Brown until the ham is shrivelled; then put the peas in, season with a pinch of pepper and very little salt, mix and complete the cooking with broth, adding a little butter.

Before serving, throw the onion away.

109

PEAS WITH CORNED BEEF

(Piselli con la carne secca)

Put on the fire a hash of corned beef, garlic, parsley and oil, season with a little salt and pepper and when the garlic is browned, put the peas in. When they have absorbed the sauce, complete the cooking with broth or, failing that, with water.

110

STUFFED TOMATOES

(Pomodori ripieni)

Select ripe middle-sized tomatoes, cut them in two equal parts and scoop out the inside seeds. Season with salt and pepper and fill the tomatoes with the following hash, in such a way as to make the stuffing come over the edge of the half tomato:

Make a hash with onion, parsley and celery, put it on the fire with a piece of butter and when it is browned, put in a small handful of dried mushrooms previously softened in water and chopped very fine: add a tablespoonful of bread crumbs soaked in milk, season with salt and pepper and let the compound simmer, moistening with water if necessary. When you take from the fire add, when it is still lukewarm, grated cheese and a beaten yolk (or two) of egg, but seeing that the compound does not become too liquid.

When the tomatoes are filled, take them in the oven with a little butter and oil mixed together and serve them as a side-dish for roast beef or steak.

The stuffed tomatoes can be made simpler with a hash of garlic and parsley mixed with bread crumbs, salt and pepper and seasoned with oil when they are in the saucepan.

111

CAULIFLOWER WITH BALSAMELLA
(Cavolfiore colla balsamella)

Remove from a good sized cauliflower the external leaves and the green ribs, make a deep cut crosswise in the stalk and cook it in salted water. Then cut it in sections and brown with butter, salt and pepper. Put it in a baking tin, throw over a small pinch of grated cheese, cover with the **balsamella** (No. 54) and brown the surface.

Serve this cauliflower as an **entremets** or as a side-dish with boiled chicken or a stew.

112

STUFFED CABBAGE
(Cavolo ripieno)

Take a big cabbage, remove the hard outside leaves, cut the stem off even with the leaves and give it half cooking in salt water. Put it upside down to drain, then open the leaves one by one until the heart is exposed and on this put the stuffing. Bring up all the leaves, close them and tie with thread crosswise.

The stuffing can be made with milk veal stewed alone, or with sweetbread or chicken liver, all chopped fine. To make it more delicate, add some **balsamella** (No 54) a pinch of grated cheese, one yolk of egg and a taste of nutmeg. Complete the cooking of the cabbage in the sauce of this stew, adding a little butter, on a low fire or in the oven kept low.

Instead of filling the whole cabbage, the larger leaves may be filled one by one, rolling and tying them.

113

SIDE-DISH OF SPINACH

(Spinaci per contorno)

After cooking the spinach in boiling water and chopping them fine, the spinach can be cooked in different ways:

1. With butter, salt and pepper, adding a little brown stock, if you have it, or a few tablespoonfuls of broth, or milk.

2. With onion sauce (onion chopped very fine) and butter.

3. With butter salt and pepper, adding a very small pinch of grated cheese.

4. With butter, a drop of olive oil and tomato sauce (No. 12) or tomato paste diluted with soup stock or water.

114

ASPARAGUS

(Sparagi)

Asparagus can be prepared in many different ways, but the simplest and best is that of boiling them and serving them seasoned with olive oil and vinegar or lemon juice. However there are other ways as, for instance, the following: Put them whole to brown a little with the green part in butter and, after seasoning them with salt, pepper and a pinch of grated cheese, pour over the melted butter when it is browned. Or else divide the white from the green part and place them as follows in a fireproof plate: Dust the bottom with grated cheese and dispose over the points of the asparagus one near the other; season with salt, pepper, grated cheese and little pieces of butter. Make another layer of asparagus and, seasoning in the same way, continue until you have them. Be moderate in the seasoning. Cross the layers of asparagus like a trestle, put on the oven and keep until the seasoning, is melted. Serve hot.

If you have some brown stock, parboil them first and complete the cooking with brown stock, adding a little bust and dusting moderately with grated cheese.

115

FISH WITH BREAD CRUMBS

(Pesce col pane grattato)

This, which can also be served as a side-dish, is made especially when you have boiled fish of good quality left over.

Cut it into little pieces, remove carefully all the bones, then put it in the **balsamella** (No. 54) and season with enough salt, grated cheese and some mushrooms chopped fine. If dried mushrooms soften in water first. Then take a fireproof plate, grease it evenly with butter and dust with bread crumbs ground fine; pour into it the fish prepared as above and cover with a thin layer of bread crumbs. Finally put over a piece of butter, brown in the oven and serve hot.

116

STEWED FISH CUTLETS

(Pesce a taglio in umido)

The fish that can be used for this dish are the tunny, the umber or grayling, the sword fish and any piece of fish of large size and good savor. A pound may be sufficient for four or five persons.

Remove the scales, clean and dry well, dip in flour and put to brown in a little oil. Remove dry, throw away the oil that remains and clean the saucepan. Make a hash, chopped very fine, with half a middle sized onion, a piece of white celery and a good pinch of parsley. Put this to brown on the fire with sufficient oil and season with salt, pepper and one whole clove. When it is browned put abundant tomato sauce (No 12) or tomato paste diluted in broth or water. Let it simmer for a while, then place the fish to complete the cooking, turning it over frequently. The fish must be served with this thick gravy that ought to be abundant.

117

WHITING WITH ANCHOVY SAUCE

(Merluzzo alla Palermitana)

Take one whiting, one pound or a little more, and trim all the fins, leaving the tail and the head. Split it to remove the bone, and season with a little salt and pepper. Turn it on the back, grease with oil, season with salt and pepper, dust with bread crumbs then lay it with two tablespoonfuls of oil on a fireproof plate or baking tin.

Take three or four good sized anchovies, bone and clean them, chop them and put on the fire with two tablespoonfuls of oil, but do not allow it to boil. With this sauce cover the back of the fish and dust it all with bread crumbs, putting also some leaves of rosemary. Bake in the oven, allowing a little crust to form over, but see that it doesn't dry up, pouring over to this purpose more oil. Before removing from the tin squeeze half a lemon over.

This dish can be served surrounded by little toast with caviar, or anchovies and butter.

118

STEWED EEL

(Anguille in umido)

For this dish it is preferable to have good sized eels that must not be skinned, but cut in small pieces.

Chop some onion and parsley, put it on the fire with oil, salt, and pepper, and when the onion is browned, add the pieces of eel. Wait until it has absorbed the taste of the onion sauce and then complete the cooking with tomato sauce (No. 12).

See that there is plenty of gravy and serve with little squares or diamonds of toast.

119

EELS WITH PEAS

(Anguille coi piselli)

Cook the eels as above with the onion sauce and when it is cooked remove it dry to cook the green peas in the sauce. The pieces of eel should be put back in the sauce to be warmed. No tomato sauce is necessary here.

120

MUSSELS WITH EGG SAUCE

(Arselle in salsa d'uovo)

A good washing with fresh water is sufficient for mussels that do not have any sand to be cleaned away. Put them on the fire with a sauce of oil, garlic, parsley and a pinch of pepper. Shake them and keep the saucepan covered seeing that they do not absorb all of the sauce. Take them out when they are open and prepare the following sauce: one or more yolks of egg, according to the quantity, lemon juice, one teaspoonful of flour, broth and some of their own juice. Cook this sauce until it becomes a smooth cream and pour it on the mussels when they are served.

121

MUSSELS WITH TOMATO SAUCE

(Arselle alla livornese)

Chop fine half an onion and put it on the fire with oil and a pinch of pepper. When the onion begins to brown add a pinch of parsley chopped not very fine and after put in the mussels with tomato sauce (No. 12) or tomato paste diluted in water. Shake them often and when they are open, put them over slices of toast prepared beforehand and arranged on a plate.

122

CODFISH

(Baccalà)

I

Freshen and soak the codfish in cold water, changing the water two or three times, or, better, keeping it for some time in a vase under running cold water. Then cut it into pieces as large as the palm of the hand and dip them in flour until they are well covered. Then put a kettle or a saucepan on the fire with plenty of oil and two or three cloves of garlic, whole but a little crushed. When the garlic begins to brown put in the codfish and brown it on both sides, stirring it often, so that it doesn't burn. Salt is not necessary, or at least only a little after tasting, but a little pepper will not be amiss. Finally pour over some tomato sauce (No. 12) or tomato paste diluted in water, let it boil a little more and serve.

123

II

The following is another way to prepare the codfish, slightly different from the preceding. Cut the codfish as above, then put it as it is in saucepan with some olive oil. Spread over it a hash of garlic and parsley and season with a pinch of pepper, oil and little pieces of butter. Cook on a good fire and turn it with care, because, not being sprinkled with flour, it breaks easily. When it is cooked, squeeze a lemon over and serve.

124

FRIED CODFISH
(Baccalà fritto)

Place the codfish on the fire—after washing as explained in No. 107—in a kettle with cold water and as salt, and as soon as the water boils, remove the codfish.

After boiling cut it in little pieces and remove all the bones. Sprinkle some flour and dip in a frying paste composed of water, flour and a little oil. Fry in oil and serve hot.

125

CODFISH CROQUETTES
(Cotolette di baccalà)

Boil as explained above and, if the quantity is one pound or a little more put together two anchovies and some parsley, chopping everything together very fine. Add some pepper, a tablespoonful of grated cheese, three or four tablespoonfuls of pap, composed of bread crumbs in large pieces, water and butter, and two eggs. Give the compound the form of several flat cutlets,dip them in beaten egg and in ground bread crumbs. Fry in oil and serve with lemon, or tomato sauce.

126

FRIED DOG-FISH

(Palombo fritto)

Cut the dogfish in slices, not very thick, and place it in a plate with beaten eggs somewhat salted. Leave for some hours until half an hour before frying, dip the slices in a mixture of bread crumbs, grated cheese, garlic and parsley chopped fine, salt and pepper. A clove of garlic is sufficient for one pound of fish. Fry in oil and serve with lemon.

127

STEWED DOG-FISH

(Palombo in umido)

Cut the dog-fish in rather big pieces and then make a hash of garlic, parsley and very little onion. Put this hash on the fire with oil and when it is sufficiently browned, put the pieces of dog-fish and season with salt and pepper. When the fish is cooked pour over some tomato sauce (No. 12), let this simmer for a while, then serve.

128

ROAST-BEEF

(Arrosto)

Although roast-beef is not an Italian dish, still it is prepared in a peculiar way by the Italians, and hence this recipe finds its place here.

To obtain a good roast-beef not less than two pounds ought to be cooked on a strong fire. It ought to be covered with good olive oil and finally with cup of soup stock which with the oil and the juice from the meat will form a rich gravy, Salt it only when it is half cooked and do it moderately, because the beef is already tasty by itself.

Put it on the fire half an hour before the soup is served and the meal begins. This will be sufficient if the piece is not very big. To ascertain the cooking prick it in the bigger part with a thin larding-pin, but not often, in order not to allow too much juice to escape. The juice must neither be of the color of the blood nor too dark.

If baked it is to be seasoned with salt, oil and a piece of butter, surrounded by raw potatoes peeled. Pour in the kettle a cup of broth or of water. If you do not like cold roast beef, cut it into slices and warm with butter and brown stock or tomato sauce.

129

ROAST VEAL

(Arrosto di vitella)

Choose for that milk veal that is to be found all the year round, although it is always better during the spring or summer.

The piece or pieces of veal can be cooked in a saucepan, slightly larded with garlic and rosemary, with oil, butter and a hash of corned beef, salt, pepper and tomato sauce. In the gravy fresh peas can be cooked.

130

POT ROAST

(Arrosto morto)

This can be done with all kinds of meats, but the best is milk veal. Take a good piece of the loins, roll it and tie with a string and put on the fire with good olive oil and butter, both in small quantity. Brown well from all sides, salt when half cooked and complete the cooking with a half cup of broth, seeing that little juice remains. If no broth is at hand, use tomato sauce, or tomato paste diluted with water. Some corned beef chopped fine can also be added.

131

POT ROAST WITH GARLIC AND ROSEMARY

(Arrosto morto coll'odore dell'aglio e del ramerino)

Cook the meat as above, but add a clove of garlic and one or two bunches of rosemary in the saucepan. When serving the roast rub the gravy through a sieve without pressing and surround the meat with potatoes or vegetables cooked apart.

The leg of lamb comes very well in this way, baked in the oven.

132

BIRDS

(Arrosto di uccelli)

The best way to cook birds, and that nearly always used by the Italians, is roasted at the spit. They must be spitted with a small slice of bread between each bird. Also wrap each bird in very thin slices of bacon, in such a way that it can be spitted with this covering. Mind to slice the bacon almost as thin as paper. Pass some oil—only once—over when they begin to brown, using a brush or a feather, and salt only once, moderately.

Put on the fire when near to be served, otherwise they may get dry and lose much of their flavor. The cooking is rapidly done if on a good fire.

133

ROAST OF LAMB

(Arrosto d'agnello)

Take a leg of lamb and season it with salt, pepper, oil and a drop of vinegar. Pierce it here and there with the point of a knife and leave it like this for several hours. Also lard it with bay leaf or rosemary to be removed when serving. The leg of lamb can be baked or, as the Italians do, cooked at the spit.

124

LEG OF MUTTON

(Cosciotto di castrato arrosto)

Before cooking see that several days elapse after the animal has been butchered. This, naturally, according to the temperature. Beat it well with a wooden mallet, then skin and remove the middle bone, without spoiling the meat. Then tie it and give it a good fire at the beginning, covering the fire when half cooked. Let it cook in its own juice and in a cup of broth strained to remove the fat; nothing else. Salt when it is almost cooked, but see that it is neither too well done nor rare, just medium. Serve with its juice apart in a sauce.

135

ROAST OF HARE

(Arrosto di lepre)

The part of the hare fitted for roast is the hind quarters, but the limbs of this game are covered with little skins that must be carefully removed, before cooking, without cutting the muscles.

Before roasting keep it soaking for twelve or fourteen hours in a liquid prepared as follows: put on the fire in a kettle three tumblers of water with half a tumbler of vinegar or less in proportion with the piece to be cooked, three of four scallions chopped fine, one or two bay-leaves, a bunch of parsley, a little salt and a pinch of pepper; make it boil for five or six minutes, cool and pour when cold over the hare. When you remove the latter from the liquid wipe it and lard it all with little pieces of good bacon.

Cook on a low fire, salt it sufficiently and grease with cream and nothing else. Never use the liver of the hare which, it is said, is very indigestible.

136

POT ROAST LARDED

(Arrosto morto lardellato)

Take a piece short and thick of beef or veal, quite tender and weighing about two pounds or a little more. Lard it with ham or bacon cut in little pieces. Tie with a string and put it in a stewpan with a piece of butter, one fourth of a middle-sized onion cut in two pieces, three or four ribs of celery half an inch thick and as many slices of carrot. Season with salt and pepper and when the meat begins to brown—turning it often—pour over one cup of water and complete the cooking on a low fire, leaving it to absorb great part of the gravy. See, however, that it doesn't dry up and become black. When you send to the table strain the juice that has remained and pour it on the meat, that may be surrounded with potatoes cut in pieces or kept whole if small, previously browned in butter or oil.

137

PIGEON SURPRISE

(Piccione a sorpresa)

The pigeon (or chicken) must be opened and stuffed with a cutlet of milk veal. Of course this cutlet must be of proportionate size. Beat it well to render it thinner and more tender, season with salt, pepper, a pinch of spices and little pieces of butter, roll it and put inside the pigeon sewing the opening. The liver and giblets of the pigeon can be cooked apart in brown stock or in butter, after being chopped. With the resulting gravy the cutlet can be smeared. In this way the different flavor of the two qualities of meat is better amalgamated.

138

STUFFED BEEF CUTLET

Braciuola di manzo ripiena)

The ingredients for this dish are a slice of beef half an inch thick, weighing about one pound, half a pound or less of lean milk veal, two small slices of ham and two or three of tongue, one scant tablespooful of grated cheese, a piece of butter, two chicken livers, one egg, a crumb of bread as large as a closed fist.

Make a hash with a small onion, a little celery, carrot and parsley, put it on the fire with the butter and when it is browned, place in the saucepan the veal cut in small pieces and the chicken livers, season with little salt and pepper and complete the cooking with a little broth. Remove the veal and chicken when cooked, and chop them fine. In the gravy that remains make a pap rather hard with the crumb of bread, moistening with broth if necessary. Now mix the chopped meat, the pap, the eggs, the cheese, the ham and tongue cut in little pieces. When the stuffing is composed thus, dip the cutlet in water, in order to stretch it better, beat it with the back of the knife and flatten with its blades. Put the stuffing inside and roll up and tie tightly with a string crosswise. Roast or bake with oil and salt.

139

STUFFED CHICKEN

(Pollo ripieno)

For a middle-sized fowl use the following ingredients: two sausages, the liver and giblets of the fowl, eight or ten chestnuts well roasted, some pieces of mushrooms, a taste of nutmeg, one egg. If, instead of a fowl, it is a turkey, double the dose.

Begin by giving the sausages and the giblets half a cooking, moistening them with a little broth if necessary. Season with a little salt and pepper on account of the sausages that already contain them. Remove them and in the gravy that remains put a crumb of bread, in order to obtain with a little broth two tablespoonfuls of thick pap. Skin the sausages, chop the chicken giblets and the giblets and grind everything together with the chestnuts, the egg and the pap; this is the stuffing with which the fowl is to be filled, to be baked afterward. It is more tasty cold than hot, and it can also be cut better.

140

CHICKEN WITH SAUCE PIQUANTE

(Pollo al diavolo)

This ought to be cooked with Cayenne pepper and served with a highly seasoned sauce, but not everybody likes that and a simpler way to cook the chicken "al diavolo" is the following:

Take a young chicken, remove the neck and the legs, open it all in front and flatten it open as much as possible. Wash and wipe dry with a towel, then put it on the grill and when it begins to brown turn it. Grease it with melted butter or with oil, using a brush, and season with salt and pepper. The later may be Cayenne pepper for those who like it. Keep turning and greasing until it is all cooked.

To prepare the sauce piquante that many like with chicken broiled in this way, put four tablespoonfuls of butter in a saucepan and when it begins to brown add two tablespoonfuls of flour and stir until it is well browned, but do not let it burn. Draw to a cooler place on the range and slowly add two cupfuls of brown stock, stirring constantly, add salt and a dash of Cayenne and let simmer for ten minutes. In another saucepan boil four tablespoonfuls of vinegar one tablespoonful of chopped onion, one teaspoonful of sugar rapidly for five minutes; then add it to the sauce and at the same time add one tablespoonful of chopped capers two tablespoonfuls of chopped pickle and one teaspooful of tarragon vinegar. Stir well and let cook for two minutes to heat the pickles. If the sauce becomes too thick dilute it with a little water.

This sauce is excellent for baked fish and all roasts and boiled meats, besides being a fitting condiment for the chicken "al diavolo".

141

CHICKEN WITH HAM

(Pollo in porchetta)

Fill a chicken with thin strips of ham, about half an inch wide. Add three cloves (or sections) of garlic, two little bunches of fennel and a few grains of pepper. Season outside with salt and pepper and cook in a saucepan with butter, or preferably bake in the oven. Sausages cut lengthwise and previously skinned can be substituted for the ham.

142

CHICKEN SAUTE'

(Pollo saltato)

Take a young chicken, remove the neck and trim the wings. Cut away the legs. Cut the chicken into six pieces. Remove some of the bones. Beat an egg with a teaspoonful of water and place in it the pieces of chicken after dipping them in flour and seasoning generously with salt and pepper. Leave the pieces in the egg until it is time for cooking. Then take the pieces one by one, sprinkle with bread crumbs and place a saucepan with a good piece of butter on the fire. When the butter begins to brown put in the pieces of chicken from the side of the skin, then turn them when browned to the other side. Let them on a good fire for about ten minutes. Serve with lemon. The chicken prepared in this way is good also when cold.

143

AFRICAN HEN

(Gallina di Faraone)

This fowl, that resembles the partridge, should not be too fresh, like all game.

The best way to cook the African hen is roasted at the spit. Put in the inside a ball of butter dipped in salt and wrap it in a piece of paper greased with butter and sprinkled with salt. This paper must be removed when the fowl is nearly cooked, and then the cooking is completed greasing with more butter and adding more salt.

144

TAME DUCK ROASTED

(Anatra domestica arrosto)

Salt it inside and bandage all the breast with slices of bacon, large and thin. Grease with oil and salt moderately when the cooking is almost complete. If you have a wild duck grease with butter, as the meat is drier.

145

TURKEY

(Tacchino)

The turkey has been imported to Europe from America, but it is nevertheless a well known dish in Italian families, although not enjoying the popularity that it has on this side of the ocean. When roasted it is generally larded moderately with little pieces of garlic and bay-leaf or rosemary and seasoned with a hash of corned beef or bacon, a little butter, salt and pepper, tomato sauce or tomato paste diluted in water. The breast, flattened until it is about half an inch thick and seasoned generously some hours before cooking with oil, salt and pepper, is excellent broiled on the grill.

146

LOIN OF PORK ROASTED

(Lombo di maiale arrosto)

The loin of pork, cut in little pieces forms an excellent roast at the spit. The pieces of pork are to be divided by little pieces of toast and greased with oil.

If the pork is to be baked, choose that piece of the loin that has its ribs and that may weigh six or eight pounds. Lard it with garlic, rosemary or bay leaf and a few cloves, but moderately, and season with salt and pepper.

This roast is very popoular in Italy, where they call it **arista.**

147

LEG OF LAMB

(Agnello all'Orientale)

This is a way to cook lamb in use in the Orient and adopted by the Italians, especially in Southern Italy. The leg of lamb is to be larded with the larding pin with slices of bacon séasoned with salt and pepper, greased with butter or milk, or milk alone and salted when half cooked.

The Arabs, who are very fond of this dish, do not lard it, as pork is forbidden by their religion, but cook it with an abundance of milk.

148

BROILED PIGEON

(Piccione in gratella)

Take a young, but fat pigeon, divide it in two parts lengthwise and flatten it well with the hands. Then put it to brown in oil for four or five minutes, just to harden the meat. Season when still hot with salt and pepper, then arrange it as follows.

Melt in the fire, without boiling it, a piece of butter and mix the liquid butter with one beaten egg. Dip the pigeon in the butter and egg and keep it until it absorbs them. Then sprinkle with bread crumbs ground fine. Cook on a grill on a a low fire and serve with a sauce or a side dish.

149

STEAK IN THE SAUCEPAN

(Bistecca nel tegame)

If you have a steak that does not appear to be too tender, put it in a saucepan with a little piece of butter and some good olive oil, with a taste of garlic and bay-leaf or rosemary. Add, if necessary, a little broth or water or tomato sauce and serve with potatoes cooked in the gravy that can be made more abundant with more broth, butter and tomato sauce.

150

VEAL KIDNEY WITH ANCHOVY

(Rognone alle acciughe)

Take a veal kidney, remove the fat, cut it open and cover with boiling water. When the water has cooled, remove the kidney, wipe with a cloth, and pass through it clean sticks to make it stay open. Season with melted butter, salt and pepper and leave it so prepared for an hour or two.

Then take another piece of butter and two or three anchovies. Clean the latter, chop and mix with the butter with the blade of a knife, making a ball. Cook the kidney on the grill, but not too much, in order to keep it tender, put it on a plate and grease when hot with the ball of butter and anchovies.

151

VEAL KIDNEY SLICED

(Rognone di vitello affettato)

Cut in thin slices one or two veal kidneys, removing the granulous part that is to be found in the middle, and put the slices in a saucepan with a piece of butter, a bunch of parsley chopped very fine together with a clove of garlic. Add a cup of hot broth; salt moderately and let it cook without boiling, until the sauce is reduced to about one third.

One tablespoonful of vinegar adds a pleasant taste to this dish.

152

BROILED MUTTON KIDNEY

(Rognone di montone alla graticola)

After washing the kidneys, remove the filmy skin that covers them and cut them in the middle without, however, detaching campletely the two parts. Season with salt and pepper, grease with oil and put them on a strong fire on the grill. After ten or twelve minutes they will be broiled. Serve hot with parsley and slices of lemon.

153

MUTTON KIDNEY FRIED

(Granelli di montone fritti)

Wash, remove the skin that covers the kidneys and cut in very thin slices. Wipe with a cloth, dip first in ground bread crumbs, then in a beaten egg mixed with melted butter, then again in the bread crumbs. This must be done rapidly, at the time of frying, otherwise the bread crumbs absorb the moisture of the kidney and make them too hard.

Melt a piece of butter in a saucepan on a strong fire and when it begins to brown, dip the slices of kidney. Turn often, sprinkle with a little parsley chopped fine, salt and serve with lemon.

154

BEEF TONGUE BOILED

(Lingua di bue lessa)

The tongue is boiled like the beef. When half cooked remove the skin, which is not nice to see and has no nutrituous elements, although it is is served with a purèe of peas, or spinach or potatoes or beans, etc. But it can be served simply with sprigs of parsley.

155

BEEF TONGUE WITH OLIVES

(Lingua di bue alle olive)

Scald the tongue and peel off the skin. Then put it back to boil until fully cooked.

Melt a piece of butter and brown half a medium sized onion cut in slices. When the onion is browned remove it from the butter and dilute in the latter a teaspoonful of flour. When the flour begins to brown, thin it with one or two cups of soup stock hot and passed through a sieve. Mix and boil for ten minutes, seasoning with salt and pepper.

When the sauce is prepared place the tongue in the saucepan containing it and let it cook again on a low fire for about an hour, turning it over frequently and keeping it moistened with the gravy. Cut some olives in a spiral to remove the stone and place it in the saucepan with the tongue. This becomes more tasty if left with the olives for one or two days.

156

STEWED BEEF TONGUE

(Lingua di bue in stufato)

Clean a fresh tongue of beef; put it in a plate,

salt it generously and put it back in the ice-box or in the pantry, until the following day.

After twenty-four hours, scald it in boiling water, skin and lard with little pieces of bacon and put it in a kettle or a large saucepan in which the seasoning is already placed. This seasoning consists of ½ lb bacon cut in very thin slices, ¼ lb. butter, one or two thin slices of ham and two middle sized onions, sliced. Sprinkle the tongue with flour, surround it with chopped meat and place the saucepan on the fire. When the tongue begins to brown, pour five or six cups of soup stock and one cup of water. Add the usual bunch of greens, two or three cloves, salt, a pinch of pepper and one of cinnamon.

Cover the saucepan tightly, boil for about four hours, rub the sauce through a sieve and serve everything hot.

157

VEAL SWEETBREADS

(Animelle di vitello)

Keep in fresh water for an hour. Then place them in a skimmer (ladle with holes) and dip in boiling water or broth. After a brief boiling remove and cool in cold water. Then remove the veins and gullet, taking care not to tear them. The sweetbreads are prepared in various ways and here we give some of the best known:

Sweetbreads with butter. — Boil in broth or

water, clean and cut into slices. Brown a piece of butter with salt and pepper. Then place the sliced sweetbreads and brown them. Before serving squeeze on a little lemon juice. The sweetbreads prepared in this way are served preferably with rice or vegetables.

Sweetbreads with white sauce. — Boiled, cleaned and cut into slices, they are placed in white sauce or **balsamella** (No. 54) adding a taste of nutmeg, pepper, salt and the juice of half a lemon.

Sweetbreads in fricassee.—Boil, trim and cut into pieces. Then brown in butter with a scallion chopped fine. Once browned, remove from the gravy in which pour a tablespoonful of flour, moistened with broth. The sauce that results is bound with egg-yolks and lemon juice.

Sweetbreads fried.—Boil and trim. Then cut in large slices, neither too thick nor too thin. Dip in beaten egg and in bread crumbs ground. Then fry in butter. Serve with vegetables.

158
TENDERLOIN WITH SPICES
(Filetto alla piemontese)

Clean and trim the meat, removing all the little skins. Then sprinkle with nutmeg, cinnamon, salt, and pepper, and place in an earthen vase covered, together with a bunch of aromatic herbs, sage, parsley, rosemary, onion, carrot and celery, all chopped fine. After a few hours melt and brown a piece of butter with the aromatic herbs, then remove the latter and place the tenderloin, leaving it to simmer for half an hour, pricking it often with a large fork or a larding pin, to add its juice to the gravy. Serve hot.

159
STUFFED ONIONS
(Cipolle ripiene)

Boil six large onions for an hour. Then drain and skin. Remove the heart with the point of a knife. In the place of the heart place the stuffing made with ¼ lb. of ham or tongue, chopped and mixed with bread crumbs ground, two tablespoonfuls of milk, two pinches of salt and one of pepper. When the onions are prepared and stuffed place them in a saucepan whose bottom has been greased with butter, sprinkle with bread crumbs ground and place in the oven, not too hot. At the time of serving add some white sauce or balsamella (No 54). Stuffed onions are served as vegetables, or side-dish with roast-beef or boiled-beef.

160
STEWED ONIONS
(Cipolle in stufato)

Keep in cold water, for half an hour, two pounds of middle-sized onions. Afterward skin and place in a saucepan in which pour as much broth as is necessary to cover them. Let them cook on a low fire for an hour, if they are scallions, or young onions. If they are not, two hours are not enough, sometimes.

When cooked and soft, drain and place in a large deep dish. Brown a piece of butter with a tablespoonful of flour, a cup of broth, salt and pepper. Mix everything and when it begins to boil pour the sauce on the onions, which must be served hot.

161
VEAL LIVER
(Fegato di vitella alla veneziana)

Brown a large onion cut in thin slices in oil and place in the saucepan the liver cut in thin slices. Brown everything on a strong fire. When the liver takes a reddish color it is ready. If it is overdone, it becomes too hard. Salt just before removing from the saucepan.

162
FRIED LIVER
(Fegato al tegame)

Clean and trim the liver, then cut in slices half an inch thick. Dip in flour and place, without delay in a saucepan in which a small onion has been browned in butter. Salt just before serving.

163
POLENTA WITH SAUSAGES
(Polenta colle salsicce)

The polenta is a very popular dish in Northern

Italy and can be prepared in various ways. Always, however, it is better to serve with the addition of sausages, or with birds or tomato paste.

The **polenta** is practically corn-meal and it is made with the so-called **farina gialla** or yellow flour.

The ingredients for a good polenta are one pound of corn meal, preferably granulous, one quart and a half of water, salted in proportion, one piece of butter, one cup and a half of milk.

Pour the meal little by little into boiling water, continually stirring with a wooden spoon. When the meal is half cooked, put the butter and pour the milk little by little. While the **polenta** boils, place on the fire in a little saucepan a tablespoonful of olive oil or a small piece of butter. When the oil is hot or the butter is melted, put some sausages repeatedly pricked with a fork.

When the sausages are cooked, pour the polenta hot in a dish and place the sausages and the gravy in a cavity practised in the middle. Serve hot.

In cooking the sausages two or three bay-leaves may be added and removed before serving.

164
SAUSAGES WITH ONIONS
(Salsicce alla cipollata)

The **salsicce alla cipollata** are prepared with fresh and lean pork meat and bacon in equal quantity, chopped fine and seasoned with salt, pepper and spices. Add a proportional quantity of onions chopped very fine, not too much, however. Fill with the hash the prepared entrails, tie every two inches to divide the sausages.

CELERY
(Sedano)

Beside being used as a condiment with a great quantity of dishes, the celery may be prepared in various different ways to form appetizing vegetable dishes. We give here a certain number of those that appear most commonly on Italian tables:

165
CELERY WITH BUTTER
(Sedano al burro)

Two heads of celery for each person.

Clean and trim, removing the sprigs that are too hard, and the leaves, that are to be cut where they begin to be green. Finally trim the stem. Then wash repeatedly in running water, drain and put to boil in salted boiling water. Remove when cooked and drain again.

About three quarters of an hour before serving, melt a piece of butter in a saucepan and brown the celery, turning them often for about ten minutes. After that pour over hot stock (soup stock or chicken broth) cover the saucepan and parboil. A few moments before serving season with brown stock, if you have any at hand, otherwise with salt and pepper only.

166

CELERY AU JUS

(Sedano al sugo)

Select nine or ten heads, neither too hard nor too soft, and cut them about four inches from the root. Remove the green and hard branches and trim the root, cutting the latter to a point. Scald the celery, after washing well, in salted boiling water. Ten minutes will be sufficient. Dip in cold water, open well the leaves and wash again carefully. Drain and make bunches of two or three heads each that you will put in a saucepan with a pint of broth or water and half a cup of good fat, onion and carrot chopped, salt and pepper. Cover and let it simmer for about two hour. Then remove the celery, drain and serve.

167

SAUCE FOR CELERY AU JUS

(Salsa per sedani al sugo)

The celery, prepared as above, are seasoned with the following sauce: Make a **roux** melting a piece of butter and browning an equal weight of flour; stir for about three minutes on the fire, after which thin the roux with a little brown stock or with bouillon cubes diluted in water. Continue stirring and reduce the sauce. Then rub through a sieve, pour over the celery and serve very hot.

168

FRIED CELERY

(Sedani fritti)

This is a convenient way to prepare left-over celery that is still too good to be thrown away.

Clean the left-over celery removing as best you can the sauce in which they were served, dip in frying paste (flour and egg) fry and serve with lemon.

169

PUREE OF CELERY

(Macco di sedani)

Take some big roots of celery, prepare as usual and wash in running water. Boil in salted water, crush and rub through a sieve. Put in a saucepan this purèe, with a piece of butter, salt, flour and a little cream or milk. The milk may be substituted with good soup stock or brown stock. Just before serving add a little powdered sugar.

170

STEW

(Stufato)

The Italian **stufato** is somewhat different from the stewed meat that is known under the name of "Irish stew". It corresponds to the French daube and is prepared in Italy in many different ways.

An excellent **stufato** can be made in the following way: Chop fine two bunches of parsley, a small carrot, half a medium sized onion, a little piece of seallion and two bay-leaves. Brown with a good piece of butter in a saucepan in which one and a half tablespoonful of oil have been previously poured.

The meat must have been prepared beforehand, that is to say washed, trimmed and larded. When half cooked, season moderately with salt and pepper. If necessary, moisten with broth or water. During the cooking the saucepan must be covered with its cover and with a sheet of paper greased with fat or oil. The stufato will be ready after about three hours' cooking on a low fire.

171
SOUTHERN STEW
(Stufato Meridionale)

Put the piece of meat in a saucepan of such a size that it remains completely filled, moisten with two cups of water and two of white wine, season with salt and pepper and cook for five hours on a low fire.

172
STEW MILANAISE
(Stufato alla milanese)

Beat and flatten a good piece of meat and lard with bacon or ham cut in small pieces. Season with salt, pepper and a taste of cinnamon. Sprinkle flour over the meat.

Place in a saucepan a little fat of beef chopped

with a middle sized onion and brown with a piece of butter. When the onion is browned, remove it and place the meat over the melted butter. Brown with melted butter. Then fill the saucepan with half water, half red wine, but only when the meat is browned from all sides. Cover the saucepan the best you can, with cover and greased paper and let it simmer for five or six hours on a very low fire.

After removing the stew, let it cool, rub the gravy through a sieve, put again on the fire and serve hot.

173

FRENCH STEW

(Stufato alla francese)

Prepare on the bottom of the saucepan a layer of thin slices of ham, on which place several little cubes also of bacon. In the middle place a bunch of parsley, and around this some cloves, half an onion sliced, a few carrots in little cubes several young onions, bay-leaf, salt, and pepper.

On this bed lay the meat that may be larded with bacon or ham and seasoned with salt, pepper and a taste of cinnamon. Pour on the meat two cups of soup stock or water and one cup of white wine. Cover the saucepan hermetically and cook on a very low fire for five hours.

When the stufato is to be served cold, the

gravy is to be rubbed through a sieve before it gets cold.

Note.— In these and similar dishes we have indicated the use of wine, which is a common ingredient, in small quantities in Italian and French cooking. This, however, can always be dispensed with if its taste is not appreciated, or for any other reason.

174

TROUT ALPINE

(Trota all'alpigiana)

These are many ways to prepare this delicious fish, found in abundance in the many streams of clear water that run from the Alps and the Apennine mountains. Often the trout is cooked in wine, but, of course, this part many be changed.

For the **trota all'alpigiana,** so called because it is the favorite dish of Piedmont, the trout must be cleaned, scaled, washed, wiped then salted and left under the action of the salt for about an hour.

Pour in a fish-kettle one quart of white wine to which will be added three medium sized onions a few cloves, two sections of garlic and a little bunch made of thyme, bay-leaf, basil or mint; finally a piece of butter as large as an egg, dipped in flour. Then put the trout in the fish-kettle and place on a strong fire. When the liquid has boiled the trout is cooked. Remove the onions and the bunch of greens and serve the trout with its gravy and some parsley.

175
TROUT LOMBARD
(Trota fritta)

Clean, scale, wash and wipe the trout. Salt and leave for half an hour. Fill with water half a fish-kettle; add half a lemon, two bay-leaves, one carrot light or ten berries of pepper, one onion divided into four parts, salt and three cloves. When the water is lukewarm, dip in the trout. Cook on a moderate fire and serve the trout with parsley, slices of lemon and young potatoes boiled. A good fish-sauce ought to accompany it.

176
FRIED TROUT
(Trota fritta)

Small and young trouts are best for frying. Scale, clean, wash and wipe. Then dip in flour and fry like the other fish in oil or in butter. Serve with browned parsley and lemon.

177
TROUT WITH ANCHOVIES
(Trota alle acciughe)

Scale, clean wash and wipe the trouts. Cut the sides and place to pickle with salt, pepper berries, garlic, parsley and onions chopped fine; with mushrooms chopped fine with thyme, bay-leaf and mint, all seasoned with good olive oil. Rub the pickled pieces at the sieve and place it and the trout in a baking-tin. Bake in the oven and serve with anchovy sauce (No. 17).

178

EGGS WITH ONION SAUCE

(Uova trippate)

Prepare some hard boiled eggs, shell and cut into disks one third of an inch thick.

Melt in a saucepan a piece of butter in which brown half an onion cut into thin slices, to be removed from the butter when browned. Then add to the butter two teaspoonfuls of flour, mix but don't allow to brown, thin with a cup of hot broth, add salt and pepper and let simmer for ten minutes. Put the sliced eggs in the sauce to warm them, stir a little, but carefully to avoid breaking them, and do not boil again. Just before serving add to the sauce a teaspoonful of cream and stir carefully.

179

EGGS WITH HAM

(Uova al prosciutto)

Place in a frying pan as many pieces of butter, large like a nut, as there are eggs to be cooked. For each piece of butter put a little slice of ham and place the frying pan on the fire. As soon as the butter is melted break an egg on each slice of ham. Let cook for ten minutes on a moderate fire.

180

EGGS WITH TOMATO SAUCE

(Uova al pomidoro)

Prepare some hard boiled eggs, cut them through the middle lengthwise, place in good order upon a plate and pour some good tomato sauce, taking care not to cover the upper part of the eggs, which must emerge from the sauce.

Instead of the tomato, the eggs may be arranged with a **balsamella** sauce (No. 54).

181

SCRAMBLED EGGS

(Uova strapazzate)

Break the eggs in a plate, assuring first that they are all fresh.

Melt in a saucepan a piece of butter about as big as an egg. When it is melted pour the egg and scramble them with a fork on a low fire.

When the eggs are cooked season moderately with salt and butter. Just when you take them away from the fire and before serving add a tablespoonful of milk or liquid cream. Serve hot with a little grated cheese.

The scrambled eggs can be served with points of asparagus, truffles, mushrooms, etc. which are prepared just as if they were to go in an omelet.

PART II

PASTRY, SWEETS, FROZEN DELICACIES, SYRUPS

182

PUDDING OF HAZELNUTS

(Budino di nocciuole)

Shell half a pound of hazelnuts in warm water and dry them well at the sun or on the fire, then grind them very fine, together with sugar, of a weight somewhat less than the nuts. Put one quart of milk on the fire, and when it begins to boil, put two third lb. lady fingers or macaroons crumbed and let it boil for five minutes, adding a small piece of butter. Rub everything through a sieve and put back on the fire with the nuts to dissolve the sugar. Let it cool and add six eggs, first the yolks, then the white beaten, pour in a mold greased with butter and sprinkled with bread crumbs ground fine. The mold must not be all full. Bake in the oven and serve cold.

This dose will be sufficient for eight or ten persons.

183

CRISP BISCUITS

(Biscotti croccanti)

One pound of flour.

Half a pound granulated sugar.

¼ lb. sweet almonds, whole and shelled, mixed to a few pine-seeds.

A piece of butter, one and a half ounce.

A pinch of anise-seeds.

Five eggs.

A pinch of salt.

Leave back the almonds and pine-seeds to add them afterward, and mix everything with four eggs, so as to use the fifth if it is necessary to make a soft dough. Divide into four cakes half an inch thick and as large as a hand, place them in a receptacle greased with butter and sprinkled with flour. Glaze the cakes with yolk of eggs. Bake in the oven, but only as much as will still permit cutting the cakes into slices, which you will do the day after, as the crust will then be softened. Put the slices back in the oven ,so that they will be toasted on both sides and you will have the crisp biscuits.

184

SOFT BISCUITS

(Biscotti teneri)

For these biscuits it would be necessary to have a tin box about four inches wide and a little less long than the oven used. In this way the biscuits will have a corner on both sides and, if cut a little more than half an inch, they will be of the right proportion. The ingredients needed are:

Flour, about two ounces.

Potato meal, a little less.

Sugar, four ounces (1/4 lb.)

Sweet almonds $1\frac{1}{2}$ ounce.
Candied orange or angelica, one ounce.
Fruit preserve, one ounce.
Three eggs.

Skin the almonds, cut them in half lengthwise and dry in the sun or at the fire. Pastry cooks usually leave them with the skin but it is much preferable to skin them. Cut in little cubes the candied fruits and the preserve.

Stir for a long while, about half an hour the sugar in the egg-yolks and a little flour then add the white of the eggs well beaten and when every thing is well beaten add the flour, letting it fall from a sieve. Mix slowly and scatter on the mixing the almonds and the cubes of candied and preserved fruit. Grease and sprinkle the tin box with flour. Bake in the oven and cut the biscuits the day after. If desired these can also be roasted on both sides.

185
BISCUITS SULTAN
(Biscotto alla sultana)

Granulated sugar, six ounces.
Flour, four ounces.
Potato meal, two ounces.
Currants, three ounces.
Candied fruits, one ounce.
Five eggs.
A taste of lemon peel.
Two tablespoonfuls of brandy.

Put first on the fire the currants and the candied fruits cut in very little cubes with as much brandy or cognac as is necessary to cover them: when it boils, light the brandy and let it burn out of the fire until the liquor is all consumed: then remove the currants and candy and let them dry in a folded napkin. Then stir for half an hour the sugar with the egg-yolks and the taste of lemon peel. Beat well the white of the eggs and pour them on the sugar and yolks. Add the flour and potato meal letting them fall from a sieve and stir slowly until everything is well mixed together. Add the currants and the pieces of candied fruits and pour the mixing in a smooth mold or in a high and round cake-dish. Grease the mold or the dish with butter and sprinkle with powdered sugar or flour. Put at once in the oven to avoid that the currants and the candied fruits fall in the oven.

186

MARGHERITA CAKE

(Pasta Margherita)

Potato meal, three ounces.

Sugar, six ounces.

Four eggs.

Lemon juice.

Beat well the egg-yolks with the sugar, add the potato meal and the lemon juice and stir everything for half an hour. Finally beat well the whites, and mix the rest, stirring continually but slowly. Pour the mixture in a smooth and round mold, greased with butter and sprinkled with powdered sugar. Put at once in the oven.

Remove from the mold when cold and dust with powdered sugar and vanilla.

187

MANTUA TART

(Torta Mantovana)

Flour, six ounces.
Sugar, six ounces.
Butter, five ounces.
Sweet almonds and pine-seeds, two ounces.
One whole egg.
Four egg-yolks.
A taste of lemon peel.

First work well with a ladle the eggs with the sugar, then pour the flour little by little, still stirring, and finally the butter, previously melted in a double steamer (bain-marie). Put the mixture in a pie-dish greased with butter and sprinkled with flour or bread crumbs ground. On top put the almonds and the pine-seeds. Cut the latter in half and cut the almonds, previously skinned in warm water, each in eight or ten pieces. This tart must not be thicker than one inch, so that it can dry well in the oven, which must not be too hot.

Sprinkle with powdered sugar and serve cold.

188

CURLY TART

(Torta ricciolina)

Sweet almonds with a few bitter ones, four ounces,
Granulated sugar, six ounces,
Candied fruits or angelica, 2½ ounces,
Butter, two ounces,
Lemon peel.

Mix two eggs with flour, flatten the paste to a thin sheet on a bread board and cut into thin noodles. In a corner of the bread board make a heap of the almonds with the sugar, the candied fruit cut in pieces and the grated lemon peel. All this cut and crush so as to reduce the mixture in little pieces. Then take a pie-dish and without greasing it, spread a layer of noodles on the bottom, then pour part of the mixture, then another layer of noodles and continue until there remains no more material, trying to have the tart at least one inch thick. When it is so prepared cover with the melted butter, using a brush to apply it evenly.

189

ALMOND CAKE

(Bocca di dama)

Granulated sugar, nine ounces,
Very fine Hungarian flour, five ounces,

Sweet almonds with some bitter ones, two ounces,
Six whole eggs and three egg yolks,
Taste of lemon peel.

After skinning the almonds in warm water and drying them well, grind or better pound them well together with a tablespoonful of sugar and mix well with the flour. Put the rest of the sugar in a deep dish with the egg yolks and the grated lemon peel (just a taste) and stir with a ladle for a quarter of an hour. In another dish beat the six whites of egg and when they have become quite thick mix them with other ingredients stirring slowly everything together.

To bake place the mixture in a baking-tin greased evenly with butter and sprinkled with powdered sugar and flour.

190

CORN MEAL CAKES

(Pasta di farina gialla)

Corn meal, seven and a half ounces,
Wheat flour, five and a half ounces,
Granulated sugar, five and a half ounces,
Butter, three and a half ounces,
Lard, two ounces,
A pinch of anise seed,
One egg.

Mix together the corn meal, the flour and the anis seed and knead with the butter, the lard and the egg that quantity that you can, forming a loaf that you will put aside. What remains is to be kneaded with water forming another loaf. Then mix the two loaves and knead a little, not much because the dough must remain soft. Flatten with the rolling pin until it becomes one quarter of an inch thick, sprinkle with flour, and cut in different sizes and shapes with thin stamps.

Grease a baking tin with lard, sprinkle, with flour, glaze with the egg, bake and dust with powdered sugar.

191
BISCUIT
(Biscotto)

Six eggs,
Granulated sugar, nine ounces,
Flour, four ounces,
Potato meal, two ounces,
Taste of lemon peel.

Stir for at least half an hour the yolks of the eggs with the sugar and a tablespoonful only of the flour and meal, using a ladle. Beat the whites of the eggs until they are quite firm, mix slowly with the first mixture and when they are well incorporated pour over from a sieve the flour and the potato meal, previously dried in the sun or on the fire.

Bake in a tin where the mixture comes about one inch and a half thick, previously greasing the tin with cold butter and sprinkle with powdered sugar mixed with flour.

In these cakes with beaten whites the following method can also be followed: mix and stir first the yolks with the sugar, then put the flour then, after a good kneading, beat the whites until they are firm, pour two tablespoonfuls to soften the mixture, then the rest little by little.

192

CAKE MADELEINE

(Pasta Maddalena)

Sugar, four and a half ounces,
Flour, three ounces,
Butter, one ounce,
Egg-yolks, four,
Whites of eggs, three,
A pinch of bi-carbonate of soda,
A taste of lemon peel.

First mix and stir the yolks with the sugar and when they have become whitish, add the flour and stir for fifteen minutes more. Mix with the butter, melting or softening it fine if it is hard and finally add the whites when they are well beaten. The flour must be previously dried in the sun or on the fire.

This cake may be given different shapes, but keep it always thin and in little volume. It can be put in little molds greased with butter and sprinkled with flour, or else in a baking tin, keeping it not more than half an inch thick, and cutting it after baking in the shape of diamonds and dusting with powdered sugar.

193

ALMOND CRISP-TART

(Croccante)

Sweet almonds, four and a half ounces.

Granulated sugar, three and a half ounces.

Skin the almonds, divide the two parts and cut each part into small pieces. Put these almonds so cut at the fire and dry them until they take a yellowish color, but do not toast. Meanwhile put the sugar on the fire in a saucepan and, when it is perfectly melted, pour the almonds hot and already sligthly browned. Now lower the fire and be careful not to allow the compound to be overdone. The precise point is known when the mixture acquires a cinnamon color. Then pour little by little in a cold mold, previously greased with butter or oil. Press with a lemon against the walls of the mold, making the mixture as thin as possible. Remove from the mold when perfectly cooled and, if it is difficult to do so, dip the mold in boiling water.

The almonds can also be dried in the sun and chopped fine, adding a small piece of butter when they are in the sugar.

194
WAFER BISCUITS
(Cialdoni)

Put in a kettle:

Flour, three ounces.

Brown sugar, one ounce.

Lard virgin, half an ounce.

Cold water, seven tablespoonfuls.

First dilute the flour and the sugar in the water, then add the lard.

Put on the fire the iron for waffles or better an appropriated iron for flattened wafers. When it is quite hot open it and place each time half a tablespoonful of the paste. Close the iron and press well. Pass over the fire on both sides, trim all around with a knife and open the iron when you see that the wafer is browned. Then detach it from one side of the iron and hot as it is roll it on the iron itself or on a napkin using a little stick. This operation must be made with great rapidity because if the wafer gets cold, it cannot be rolled.

Should the wafers remain attached to the iron, grease it from time to time, and if they are not firm enough, add a little flour.

These wafer-biscuits are generally served with whipped cream.

195

QUINCE CAKE

(Cotognata)

The ingredients are about six pounds of quinces and four pounds of granulated sugar.

Put on the fire the apples covered with water, and when they begin to crack remove them, skin and scrape to put together all the pulp. Rub the latter through a sieve. Put back the pulp on the fire with the sugar and stir continually in order that it may not attack to the bottom of the kettle. It will be enough to boil for seven or eight minutes and remove when it begins to form pieces when lifted with the ladle.

Now in order to prepare the quince-cake spread it on a board to the thickness of about a silver dollar and dry it in the sun covered with cheese cloth to keep away the flies. When it is dry cut it in the form of chocolate tablets and remove each piece from the board passing the blade of a knife underneath.

If it is wished to make it crisp, melt about three and a half pounds of granulated sugar with two tablespoonfuls of water and when the sugar has boiled enough to "make the thread" smear every one of the little quince cakes with it. If the sugar becomes too hard during the operation put it back on the fire with a little water and make it boil again. When the sugar is dry on one side and on the edge, smear the other side.

196

PORTUGUESE CAKE

(Focaccia alla Portoghese)

Sweet almonds, five ounces.

Granulated sugar, five ounces.

Potato meal, one and a half ounce.

Three eggs.

One big orange or two small.

First mix the yolks of the eggs with the sugar, then add the flour, then the almonds skinned and chopped fine, then the orange juice (through a colander) then a taste of orange peel. Finally add to the mixture the whites of the eggs well beaten. Put in a paper mold greased evenly with butter, with a thickness of about an inch and bake in a very moderately hot oven. After baked, cover with a white glaze or frost, made with powdered sugar, lemon juice and the white of eggs.

197

MACAROONS

(Amaretti)

I

Granulated sugar, nine ounces.

Sweet almonds, three and a half ounces.

Bitter almonds, half of the above quantity.

Whites of egg, two.

Skin and dry the almonds, then chop them very fine. Mix the sugar and the whites of egg and stir for about half an hour, then add the almonds to form a rather hard paste. Of this make little balls, as large as a small walnut. If the paste is too soft add a little butter, if too hard add a little white of egg, this time beaten. Were it desired to give the macaroons a brownish color, mix with the paste a little burnt sugar.

As you form the little ball, that you will flatten to the thickness of one third of an inch, put them over wafers or on pieces of paper or in a baking tin greased with butter and sprinkled with half flour and half powdered sugar. Dispose them at a certain distance from one another as they will enlarge and swell, remaining empty inside.

Bake in an oven moderately hot.

II

Powdered sugar, ten and a half ounces.

Sweet almonds, three ounces.

Bitter almonds, one ounce.

Two whites of egg.

Skin the almonds and dry them in the sun or on the fire, then chop and grind very fine with one white of egg poured in various times. When this is done, put half of the sugar, stirring and kneading with your hand. Then pour everything in a large bowl and, always mixing, add half of the other white of egg, then the other half of the sugar and finally the other half of the white.

In this way an homogenous mixture will be obtained of the right firmness. Shake into a kind of a stick and cut it in rounds all equal, one third of an inch thick. Take them up one by one with moistened fingers and make little balls as large as a walnut. Flatten them to the thickness of a third of an inch and for the rest proceed as said above, but dust with powdered sugar before putting in a hot oven.

With this dose about thirty macarons can be obtained.

198

FARINA CAKES

(Pasticcini di semolino)

Farina, six and a half ounces.
Sugar, three and a half ounces.
Pine-seeds, two ounces.
Butter, a small piece.
Milk, one quart.
Four eggs.
A pinch of salt.
Taste of lemon peel.

Cook the farina in the milk and when it begins to thicken pour the pine-seeds, previously chopped fine and pounded with the sugar, then the butter and the rest, less the eggs which must be put in last when the mixture has completely cooled. Then place the whole well mixed in little molds, greased evenly with butter and sprinkled with bread crumbs ground fine, and bake.

199

RICE TART

(Torta di riso)

Milk, one quart.

Rice, seven ounces.

Sugar, five and a half ounces.

Sweet almonds with four bitter ones, three and a half ounces.

Candied cedar (angelica), one ounce.

Three whole eggs.

Five egg-yolks.

Taste of lemon peel.

A pinch of salt:

Skin the almonds and grind or pound them with two tablespoonfuls of the sugar.

Cut the candied cedar in very small cubes. Cook the rice in the milk until it is quite firm, put in all the ingredients except the eggs, which are added when the mixture is cold. Put the entire mixture in a baking tin greased with butter and sprinkled with bread crumbs ground fine, harden in the oven and after 24 hours cut the tart into diamonds. When serving dust with powdered sugar.

200

FARINA TART

(Torta di semolino)

Milk, one quart.

Farina finely ground, four and a half ounces.

Sugar, four and a half ounces.

Sweet almonds with three bitter, three and a half ounces.
Butter, a small piece.
Four eggs.
Taste of lemon peel.
A pinch of salt.

Skin the almonds in warm water and ground or pound very fine with all the sugar, to be mixed one tablespoonful at a time.

Cook the farina in the milk and before removing from the fire add the butter and the almonds, which will dissolve easily, being mixed with the sugar. Then put the pinch of salt and wait until it becomes lukewarm to add the eggs that are to be beaten whole previously. Pour the mixture in a baking tin greased evenly with butter, sprinkled with bread crumbs and of such a size that the tart has the thickness of an inch or less. Put it in the oven, remove from the mold when cold and serve whole or cut into sections.

201
PUDDING OF RICE MEAL
(Budino di farina di riso)

Milk, one quart.
Rice meal, seven ounces.
Sugar, four and a half ounces.
Six eggs.
A pinch of salt.
Taste of vanilla.

First dissolve the rice meal in half a pint of the milk when cold, and pour it in the rest of the milk when it is boiling. This is done to prevent the formation of lumps. When the meal is cooked add the sugar, the butter and the salt. Remove from the fire and when it is lukewarm mix the eggs (beaten) and the taste of vanilla. Then bake the pudding like all the others and serve warm.

202

BREAD PUDDING

(Budino di pane)

Soft bread crumb, five ounces.

Butter, three and a half ounces.

Four eggs.

Taste of lemon peel.

A pinch of salt.

Cut the bread crumb into pieces and soak in cold milk. Then rub though a sieve. Melt the butter in a double boiler (in a vessel immersed in boiling water) and mix with the eggs until butter and eggs are incorporated to each other. Add the bread crumb and the sugar and mix well. Pour the mixture in a mold greased with butter and sprinkled with bread crumb ground fine and bake like other puddings.

203

POTATO PUDDING

(Budino di patate)

Potatoes, big and mealy, one and a half lb.

Sugar, five and a half ounces.
Butter, one and a half ounces.
Flour, a tablespoonful.
Milk, half a pint.
Six eggs.
A pinch of salt.
Paste of cinnamon or lemon peel.

Boil or steam the potatoes, skin and rub through a sieve. Place them back again on the fire with the butter, the flour and the milk, all poured little by little, stirring well with the ladle, then add the sugar, the salt and the cinnamon or lemon peel (just a taste) and mix everything together well. Remove from the fire and, when the mixture is lukewarm or cold add the eggs, first the yolks, then the whites beaten.

Bake like all other puddings and serve hot.

204

LEMON PUDDING
(Budino di limone)

One big lemon.
Sugar, six ounces.
Sweet almonds with 3 bitter ones, six ounces.
Six eggs.

Cook the lemon in water, for which two hours will be enough. Remove dry and rub through a sieve. Before rubbing, however, taste it, because if it has a bitter taste it must be kept in cold water until it has lost that unpleasant taste. Add the sugar, the almonds skinned and ground very fine and the six yolks of the eggs. Beat the whites of the eggs and add them to the mixture that will then be put in a mold and baked like all other puddings.

205
PUDDING OF ROASTED ALMONDS
(Budino di mandorle tostate)

Milk, one quart.
Sugar, three and a half ounces.
Sweet almonds, two ounces.
Lady-finger biscuits, two ounces.
Three eggs.

First prepare the almonds, that is to say skin them in warm water and toast them on the fire over a plate of iron or a stone, then grind very fine. Boil the sugar and the lady-fingers, broken in little pieces in the milk, mixing well. After half an hour of boiling, keeping always stirred, rub the mixture through a sieve. Then add the toasted and ground almonds. When it is cold add the beaten eggs, pour it in a smooth mold, whose bottom will be covered with a film of liquified sugar and cook in a double boiler, that is to say put the mold well closed in a kettle full of boiling water.

When cooked let it cool and place in ice-box before serving.

206

CRISP CAKE IN DOUBLE BOILER

(Croccante a bagno maria)

Sugar, five and a half ounces.
Sweet almonds, three ounces.
Egg-yolks, five.
Milk, one pint.

Skin the almonds and chop them in little pieces about as big as a grain of wheat. Put on the fire two thirds of the sugar and when it is all melted pour the almonds and stir continually with the ladle until they have taken the color of cinnamon. Then put them in a tin greased with butter and when they are cold, pound them very fine with the remaining third of sugar.

Add the yolks and then the milk, mix well and pour the mixture in a mold with a hole in the middle and greased evenly with butter. Place the mold in a double boiler so that it will be cooked by steam.

206

STUFFED PEACHES

(Pesche ripiene)

Six big peaches not very ripe.
Four or five lady-finger biscuits.
Granulated sugar, three ounces.
Two ounces sweet almonds with three peach kernels.
Candied fruit (angelica) half an ounce.

Cut the peaches in two parts, remove the stones and enlarge somewhat the cavity where they were with the point of a knife. Mix the peach pulp that you extract with the almonds, already skinned, and grind the pulp and almonds very fine together with two ounces of the sugar. To this mixture add the lady-fingers crumbed and the candied fruits. Cut in very small cubes. This will be the stuffing with which you will fill the cavities of the twelve halves of peach. These you will place in a row in a baking tin, with the stuffing above. Add the remaining ounce of sugar and bake in oven with a moderate fire.

207

MILK GNOCCHI

(Gnocchi di latte)

One quart of milk.
Sugar, nine ounces.
Starch in powder, four ounces.
Eight yolks of eggs.
A taste of vanilla.

Mix everything together as you would do for a cream and put on the fire in a saucepan, continually stirring with a ladle. When the mixture has become hard keep it a few moments more on the fire and then pour it in a plate to make it about half an inch thick and cut it into diamonds when it is cold. Put these diamonds one over the other with symmetry in a baking tin or in a fireproof glass plate, with some little pieces of butter in between and brown them a little in the oven. Serve hot.

208

SABAYON

(Zabaione)

Yolks of three eggs.

Granulated sugar, two ounces.

Marsala or sherry wine, five tablespoonfuls.

A dash of cinnamon.

First stir with the ladle the yolks and the sugar until they become almost white, then add the wine. When ready to serve, place the saucepan in another one containing hot water and beat until the sugar is melted and the egg begins to thicken.

SYRUPS

(Sciroppi)

The syrups of acidulated fruits, diluted with ice water are refreshing and pleasant beverages, greatly appreciated during the summer months. It is well, however, not to drink them until the digestion is completed, because they may disturb it, on account of the sugar that they contain.

209

RED CURRANT OR GOOSEBERRY SYRUP

(Sciroppo di ribes)

Remove the stems from the bunches of gooseberry and place them in an earthen vase, to be kept in a cool place. When it has begun to ferment (which may happen after three or four days) sink the surface film and stir with a ladle twice a day, continuing this operation until it has stopped raising. Then put in a cheese cloth, letting the juice come out through pressing with the hands or in a machine. Pass the juice through a filter, two or three times if necessary, until you obtain a limpid liquid. Then put it on the fire and when it begins to boil pour in it granulated sugar and citric acid in the following proportions:

Liquid, six pounds.
Sugar, eight pounds.
Citric acid, one ounce.

That is to say for each three parts of the liquid, add four parts of sugar, and one ounce of citric acid for eight pounds of sugar mixed with six pounds of liquid.

Stir continually with the ladle so that the sugar does not stick to the bottom, taste it to add some more citric acid if you judge it necessary, then let it cool and place in bottles to be sealed.

When a beverage is to be prepared pour in a tumbler less than half an inch of syrup for a tumblerful of ice water.

210
RASPBERRY SYRUP
(Sciroppo di lampone)

This is prepared like the other explained above but, since this fruit contains less gluten than the gooseberry the period of fermentation will be briefer. The large quantity of sugar used in these syrups is necessary for their conservation and the citric acid is used to correct the excessive sweetness.

211
LEMON SYRUP
(Sciroppo di limone)

Three big lemons.

One and a half pound of sugar.

A tumbler of water.

Skin the lemons, removing the internal pulp without squeezing it and taking off all seeds.

Put the water on the fire with the skin of one of the lemons cut in a thin ribbon like strip with a small knife. When the water is near boiling put in the sugar then remove the lemon skin and immerse the pulp of the three lemons. Boil until the syrup is condensed and cooked right, which is known by the pearls that it makes boiling and the color of white wine that is acquires. Preserve in a bottle, and when needed, dilute in a tumbler of ice water. A small quantity will make a delightful beverage.

212

HARD BLACK-BERRY SYRUP

(Sciroppo di amarena)

Use hard but ripe black berries. They must be of the sour kind but, as said, they must not be unripe. Remove the stems and put the berries into a vase with a good piece of whole cinnamon. The fermentation will happen after 48 hours and as soon as the berries begin to rise, stir them from time to time. Then press them to extract the juice, with a pressing machine if you have one, or with your hands, squeezing them a few at a time in cheese cloth.—When the liquid has rested for a while, filter it until it becomes quite clear. When it has been depurated, put it on the fire in the following proportion and with the piece of cinnamon that was already immersed ın the cherries: Twelve pounds of liquid to sixteen pounds of sugar and two ounces of citric acid, or three parts of liquid to four of sugar and the citric acid as in the above proportion.

Before putting in the sugar and the citric acid wait until the liquid is quite hot, just before boiling. Then stir continually. The boiling must be brief, four or five minutes are sufficient to incorporate the sugar in the liquid.

When removing the syrup from the fire, put it in an earthen vase and bottle when quite cold. Cork the bottles well and keep in a cool place.

213

ORGEAT

(Orzata)

Sweet almonds with 10 or 12 bitter ones, seven ounces.

Water, one and half pounds.

Granulated sugar, two pounds.

Skin the almonds and grind them very fine, or better pound them in a mortar, moistening from time to time with orange flower water, of which you will use about two tablespoonfuls.

When the almonds have been reduced to a paste, dissolve the latter in one third of the water and filter the juice through a cheese cloth, squeezing hard. Put the paste, back in the grinder or in the mortar, grind or pound again, then filter again with another third of the water. Repeat the same operation for a third time, then put on the fire the liquid so obtained and just before boiling put the sugar, mix, stir and boil for about twenty minutes. Let it cool, then bottle and keep in a cool place. The orgeat does not ferment and the thick liquid may be diluted in water, half an inch for a whole tumbler of iced water.

214

APRICOT MARMALADE

(Conserva di albicocche)

Use good and ripe apricots. It is a mistake to believe that jam or marmalade can be obtained with any kind of fruit. Take off the stones, put them on the fire without water and while they boil, stir with a ladle to reduce them to pulp. When they have boiled for about half an hour, rub them through a sieve to separate the pulp of the fruit from the skins that are to be thrown away, then put them back on the fire with granulated sugar in the proportion of eight tenths, that is to say eight pounds of sugar for ten pounds of apricot pulp. Stir often with the ladle until the mixture acquires the firmness of marmalade, which will be known by putting from time to time a teaspoonful in a plate and seeing that it flows slowly.

When ready, remove from the fire, let it cool, and then put in vases well covered and with a film of paraffine or tissue paper dipped in alcohol, so that the air may not pass in.

215

PRESERVE OF QUINCE

(Conserva di cotogne soda)

The ingredients are quinces, peeled and with the core removed, and granulated sugar, in the proportion of eight tenths of quinces to five tenths of sugar, or a little more than one and a half quinces for one part of sugar.

Dissolve the sugar on the fire with half a glass of water, boil a little, then remove from the fire and put aside.

Cut the quinces—peeled and coreless—in very thin slices and put them on the fire with a glass of water, supposing the quantity to be about two pounds. Keep covered, but stir once in a while with the ladle, trying to break the slices and reduce them to a paste. When the quinces are made tender through cooking, pour in the thick syrup of sugar already prepared, mix and stir and let the mixture boil with the cover removed until the preserve is ready, which will be known when it begins to fall like shreds when taken up with the ladle.

Let it cool and put in well covered jars.

ICES

(Gelati)

Although it is in America that there is a greater consumption of ice cream, it is in Italy that it was first made, and in various European capitals it is the Italian **gelatiere** who prepares the frozen delicacy. A few Italian recipes of **gelati** will then be acceptable, we believe, as a conclusion to this little work.

216

BISCUIT

(Pezzo in gelo)

Make a cream with:

Water, five ounces.

Sugar, two ounces.

The yolks of four eggs.

A taste of vanilla.

Put it on the fire stirring continually and when it begins to stick to the ladle remove from the fire and whip to a stiff froth. Then mix about five ounces of ordinary whipped cream, put in a mold and pack in salt and ice.

Keep in ice for about three hours.

This dose will be sufficient for seven or eight persons.

217.

LEMON ICE

(Gelato di limone)

Granulated sugar, ¾ lb.

Water, a pint.

Lemons, three (good sized).

Boil the sugar in the water, with some little pieces of lemon peel, for about ten minutes, in an uncovered kettle. When this syrup is cold, squeeze the lemons one at the time, tasting the mixture to regulate the degree of acidity. Then strain and put in the freezer packed with salt and ice.

218

STRAWBERRY ICE

(Gelato di fragola)

Ripe strawberries, ¾ lb.
Granulated sugar, ¾ lb.
Water, one pint.
A big lemon.
An orange.

Boil the sugar in the water for ten minutes in an uncovered kettle. Rub through a sieve the strawberries and the juice of the lemon and the orange: add the syrup after straining, mix everything and pour the mixture in the freezer.

219

ORANGE ICE

(Gelato di aranci)

Four big oranges.
One lemon.
One pint of water.
Sugar, ¾ lb.

Squeeze the oranges and the lemon and strain the juice.

Boil the sugar in the water for ten minutes, put in the juice when cold, strain again and put in the freezer.

220

PISTACHE ICE CREAM

(Gelato di pistacchi)

Milk, one quart.

Sugar, six ounces.

Pistaches, two ounces.

Skin the pistaches in warm water and grind them very fine with a tablespoonful of the sugar, then put in a saucepan with the yolks and the sugar, mixing everything together. Add the milk and put the mixture on the fire stirring with the ladle and when it is condensed like cream, let it cool and put in the freezer.

221

TUTTI FRUTTI

To make this ice a special ice cream mold is necessary, or a tin receptacle that can be closed hermetically.

Take several varieties of fruits of the season, ripe and of good quality, that is to say, strawberries, cherries, plums, apricots, a big peach, a good sized pear, a piece of good cantaloupe. Peel, skin and remove stones and cores of all these fruits. Then cut them into very thin slices, throwing away the cores and stones.

When the fruit is prepared in this manner, weigh it, and sprinkle over one fifth of its weight of powdered sugar, squeezing also one lemon. Mix everything and let the mixture rest for half an hour.

Put a sheet of paper in the bottom of the mold that is to be filled with the fruit pressed together, close, and pack in salt and ice, keeping it for two hours or a little less.

This is not the **tutti frutti** ice cream as is known in America, but a **macèdoine** of fruits, that comes very pleasant to the taste in the summer months.

INDEX

NUMBERS REFER TO RECIPES

INDEX, *continued*